THE PSALMS

THE PSALMS

in Rhythmic Prose

Translation based on the authorized
Latin version rendered from the
original texts by members of the
Pontifical Biblical Institute

TRANSLATED BY

JAMES A. KLEIST, S.J., Ph.D.

QUONDAM PROFESSOR OF CLASSICAL LANGUAGES
SAINT LOUIS UNIVERSITY

AND

THOMAS J. LYNAM, S.J.

ASSOCIATE PROFESSOR OF RELIGION
SAINT LOUIS UNIVERSITY

THE BRUCE PUBLISHING COMPANY
MILWAUKEE

IMPRIMI POTEST:
    DANIEL H. CONWAY, S.J.
    Praep. Prov. Missourianae
NIHIL OBSTAT:
    ROBERT G. BOUCHER, C.Ss.R., S.T.L., S.S.L.
    Censor Deputatus
IMPRIMATUR:
    ✠ ALBERTUS G. MEYER
    Archiepiscopus Milwauchiensis

August 6, 1954

Preface

The Reverend James A. Kleist, S.J., enjoyed a well-merited reputation in the field of classical languages. Over an extensive period of years, his books and articles were welcomed by authorities in that department of learning.

Some two years before his death, Father Kleist asked the present writer to collaborate with him in translating the Psalms from the new Latin version recently brought out by the scholars of the Pontifical Biblical Institute. In particular, he wanted a colleague to act as consultant in deciding the ultimate English expression into which the Psalms were to be cast, to prepare an analysis of each Psalm, and to supply any notes needed.

Father Kleist's plan, which was gladly accepted, was to do the Psalms in rhythmic prose, and in that medium they are presented in this volume. The Psalms form the very heart of the old Hebrew poetry. But in this version the translators do not attempt to present them as poetry, in the sense in which that term is used in English literature. We use prose, but we do make a borrowing from poetry, in that the prose has introduced into it a stress, a rhythm. There is no intention, therefore, of a metrical rendition; a merely rhythmical rendition is presented. The iambic was chosen since that is the stress most commonly used in English poetry. Hence, it will be found that the movement of the Psalms in this translation is essentially iambic, with the occasional and natural substitution of an anapaest.

A final revision and polishing of the text had been agreed upon. Father Kleist's death, however, intercepted this plan. Thus the completion of the work on the manuscript had to be carried out without the benefit of his assistance.

This version of the Psalms is offered as a book for meditative reading and prayer. For this reason, footnotes and other scholarly apparatus have been kept to a very minimum.

The analysis preceding each Psalm and the selected notes are translated from the version of the Pontifical Biblical Institute, whose Rector, the Reverend Ernest Vogt, S.J., graciously gave permission for this use.

I must not fail to mention my debt to the late Father Joseph Husslein, S.J., who for many years was the distinguished editor of the "Science and Culture Series." Father Husslein was constant in his encouragement during the various early stages of this project.

I am also indebted to my confrere, the Reverend Raymond E. Bernard, S.J., of the editorial staff of *Social Order*, for a final reading of the proofs and other valuable assistance.

THOMAS J. LYNAM, S.J.

Saint Louis University
June 25, 1954

Contents

Preface v

BOOK 1: Psalms 1–40

PSALM

1. Two Modes of Life 3
2. The Messias, King of Sion and of All the Earth . . 3
3. Trust in God, in the Midst of Enemies 4
4. Trust in God, in the Midst of Unbelieving Sinners . 5
5. Morning Prayer of a Good Man in the Midst of Enemies 6
6. Prayer of a Man Chastised by God 7
7. An Appeal to God, the Judge, by One Falsely Accused 8
8. The Majesty of God; the Dignity of Man . . . 10
9A. Thanksgiving for Victory Over the Gentiles . . . 11
9B. Against Oppressors of the People 12
10. A Good Man's Stanch Confidence in God . . . 14
11. Against Proud and Treacherous Enemies 14
12. The Psalmist's Trust in God 15
13. The World's Corruption; Its Punishment . . . 16
14. Who Dares Appear Before the Lord? 17
15. God, Our Greatest Good; the Source of Resurrection and Eternal Life 17
16. A Plea for Help Against Powerful Foes 18
17. David Thanks God for Saving Him 20
18. Praise of God, the Creator and Lawgiver 23
19. Prayer for the King as He Goes to War 25
20. God's Manifold Blessings to David; the Israelites' Gratitude 26
21. The Passion of the Messias and Its Fruit 27
22. The Lord Is My Shepherd 29
23. Solemn Entry of the Lord Into His Holy Place . . 30
24. Petition for Forgiveness and Freedom From All Troubles 31

PSALM

25. The Psalmist, Falsely Accused, Turns to God for Judgment. 33
26. Undaunted Trust in God 34
27. A Prayer of Supplication and Thanksgiving . . . 35
28. The Majesty of God Seen in the Tempest . . . 36
29. Thanksgiving for Deliverance From Death . . . 37
30. An Appeal in Time of Great Distress; Thanksgiving for Answered Prayer 38
31. Happy the Man Whose Sin Has Been Pardoned . . 41
32. Praise of the Power and Providence of God . . . 42
33. Fear of God and Its Reward 43
34. A Petition for Help Against Unjust and Ungrateful Persecutors 45
35. On Human Wickedness and Divine Providence . . 47
36. The Lot of Good Men and That of Evil Ones . . 48
37. Prayer of a Sinner Afflicted by God 51
38. Laments and Prayers of a Seriously Sick Man . . . 52
39. Thanksgiving and a Prayer for Aid in a New Affliction 54
40. Confidence and Prayer of a Sick Man 56

BOOK 2: Psalms 41–71

41 and 42. The Desire to Be With God in His Holy Temple 61
43. The People of Israel, Once Protected by God, but Now Repudiated by Him, Seek His Help . . . 63
44. A Nuptial Song for the King, the Messias . . . 65
45. God, Our Defense and Strength 66
46. God, the Victorious King, Ascends His Throne . . 67
47. God's Glory Manifested in the Deliverance of the Holy City 68
48. Men Wonder at the Prosperity of Sinners . . . 70
49. Concerning the Right Worship of God 71
50. Confession of a Penitent Sinner; His Promises and Petitions 73
51. Against a Rich and Influential Calumniator . . . 75
52. The Depravity of All Men and Their Punishment . 76
53. A Prayer for God's Help Against Enemies . . . 77

CONTENTS

ix

PSALM

54. Against His Enemies and a Certain Faithless Friend . 78
55. When Oppressed, the Psalmist Places Full Trust in God 80
56. In the Midst of Persecution, the Psalmist Is All Trustful 81
57. A Rebuke for Unjust Judges 82
58. Against Grasping and Bloodthirsty Enemies . . . 83
59. Lamentation, Confidence, Prayers After a Disaster Suffered by the People 85
60. The King Prays; He Is Heard; He Exults 86
61. In God Alone We Place Our Trust 87
62. Longing for God, Our Life and Our Salvation . . 89
63. God's Judgment on Treacherous Persecutors . . . 90
64. Solemn Thanksgiving for the Blessings of God . . 91
65. A Hymn for a Sacrifice of Thanksgiving 92
66. A Blessing Is Asked Upon the Work of Spreading the Faith Among the Gentiles 94
67. Triumphal Journey of the Ark From Egypt to Mount Sion 95
68. Prayer of a Man Who Is Grievously Afflicted for the Sake of God 98
69. A Petition for Divine Help 101
70. "Do Not Discard Me in My Age" 102
71. The Messianic Kingdom 104

BOOK 3: Psalms 72–88

72. Problem of the Prosperity of the Wicked and Its Solution 109
73. Lamentation and Prayers Over the Devastated Temple 111
74. The Lord Is a Just Judge 113
75. Triumphal Song After a Great Victory 114
76. The People Are Afflicted; Their Consolation, Their Solace 115
77. The Blessings of God; the Ingratitude of the People of Israel 117
78. Lamentation Over the Destruction of Jerusalem . 122
79. "Protect the Vine" 123
80. A Hymn and a Warning on a Solemn Feast Day . . 125

CONTENTS

PSALM

81. The Final End of Unjust Judges 127
82. Against Enemies Joined to Oppose the Israelites . . 128
83. The Psalmist's Longing for the Temple 129
84. "His Redemption Is at Hand" 130
85. Prayer of a Good Servant of God When in Trouble . 132
86. Sion, the Fatherland of All Peoples 133
87. Prayer of a Man Seriously Ill 134
88. Ruin of the House of David Compared With the
Promises God Once Made to David 136

BOOK 4: Psalms 89–105

89. Man's Life Is Brief; Let the Eternal God Be His
Refuge Always 143
90. The All-High God, Protector of the Just 144
91. Praise of God as Wisely and Justly Governing Human
Affairs 146
92. The Lord Is Powerful King of the World 147
93. God Is Invoked for Help Against Wicked Oppressors 148
94. A Call to Praise God and Render Him Obedience . 149
95. Praise God, King of All the Earth 150
96. The Lord Confounds the Worshipers of False Gods;
the True of Heart He Praises 152
97. The Lord Is Victor, King, and Just Judge 153
98. The Holiness of the King 154
99. Hymn Sung When Entering the Temple . . . 155
100. Resolutions of a Model Ruler 156
101. Lament and Prayers of One in Anguish 157
102. Praises of God's Mercy 159
103. Praise of God, the Creator 161
104. God's Promises to Abraham Are Fulfilled . . . 164
105. The Sins of an Ungrateful People; Their Chastisements 167

BOOK 5: Psalms 106–150

106. Thanksgiving for Deliverance From Perils . . . 173
107. Praise of God and a Petition for His Aid in War . . 176
108. Against Unjust and Relentless Enemies 177

CONTENTS

PSALM

109. The Messias, Priest, King, Victor 179
110. God's Splendid Works in Israel 180
111. The Happiness of a Good Man 181
112. Praise of the All-High and All-Merciful God . . . 182
113A. The Marvels Worked by God During the Exodus 183
113B. Greatness and Goodness of the True God . . . 184
114 and 115. Thanksgiving of a Man Saved From Death . 186
116. Hymn of Praise and Thanksgiving 188
117. Thanksgiving for the Nation's Safety 188
118. Praise of the Law 191
119. A Protest Against Wicked Tongues 203
120. God, the Preserver and Protector of His Temple . . 204
121. A Salute to Jerusalem, the Holy City 205
122. A Contemned People's Trust in God 206
123. It Is the Lord Who Saves Us From Extreme Danger . 206
124. God Is the Helper of His People Against Their Enemies 207
125. A Prayer for the Total Restoration of the People . . 208
126. All Prosperity Is a Blessing of God 209
127. Domestic Happiness of a Good Israelite 209
128. Israel, Assailed From Its Youth, Implores the Aid of
     God 210
129. Man's Sins; God's Mercy 211
130. With Childlike Simplicity, the Psalmist Seeks Rest in
     God 212
131. David's Promises to God; God's Promises to David . 213
132. Joy of Fraternal Harmony 214
133. Evensong in the Temple 215
134. Praise of God, Lord of All Things and Benefactor of
     His People Israel 216
135. Thanksgiving for the Manifold Blessings of God . . 217
136. Grief and Longings of the Exiles 219
137. Thanksgiving for a Blessing 220
138. God Is Present Everywhere, Sees All Things . . . 221
139. Against Violent and Base Enemies 223
140. Prayer of a Just Man Against the Deceits of the
     Wicked 224
141. Cry of a Man Who Is Abandoned by All 225
142. Prayers of a Penitent Man Who Is in Dire Straits . 226

CONTENTS

PSALM

143. Prayers of the King for Victory and Prosperity . . 228
144. Greatness and Goodness of God 229
145. Praise of God, Eternal King and Helper of All . . 231
146 and 147. Praise of God, the Mighty and Wise Restorer
    of Israel 232
148. Let Heaven and Earth Praise the Lord 233
149. With Song and Sword Let Israel Praise the Lord . . 235
150. A Solemn Concert of Praise for God 236

BOOK 1: Psalms 1-40

Psalm 1

Two Modes of Life

The psalmist describes two modes of life and the outcome of each.
I. The way of the good (1–3). II. The way of the wicked (4–6).

I   **1**   O well for him who does not follow
the counsel of godless men,
nor enters on the sinners' path,
nor is a member of a scoffers' clique,
  2   but whose delight is in the law of the Lord,
who cons his law by day and night.
  3   For like is he unto a tree
by meadow rills planted,
which yields its fruit at its due time,
whose leafage does not fade.
Success attends his every enterprise.

II   **4**   Not thus the godless fare! Not thus!
Like chaff are they — chaff scattered by the wind.
  5   Therefore the godless will not stand their ground when judgment comes,
nor will the sinners, when the saints convene.
  6   The Lord takes care of the way of the good;
the way of godless men ends in the pit.

Psalm 2

The Messias, King of Sion and of All the Earth

I. The Gentiles rebel against God and the Messias (1–3). II. God
speaks to them; they are terror-stricken (4–6). III. The Messias
announces that he has been constituted universal king (7–9). IV. The
psalmist warns the rulers of the world: let them fear God or else
experience his wrath (10–12).

I   **1**   Why are the Gentiles blustering?
Why do the nations scheme in vain?

3

2 The kings of earth united rise
and princes all at once conspire
against the Lord, against his Christ:
3 "Come, let us break their bonds
and fling away from us their chains!"

II 4 But he that dwells in heaven — laughs!
The Lord — he mocks at them!
5 Then in his wrath he speaks to them,
and in his rage strikes terror into them:
6 "But I — I have installed my king
on Sion, on my holy hill!

III 7 And I will spread the Lord's decree:
the Lord has said to me: 'My Son you are: this day have I
begotten you!
8 Demand of me: the nations will I give you for a heritage;
the very bounds of earth for you to have and hold.
9 You are to rule them with an iron rod,
and shatter them like earthenware!' "

IV 10 And now, O kings, be wise!
Be lessoned, rulers of the earth!
11 Serve the Lord in fear; acclaim him joyfully;
12 pay homage to him tremblingly;
or else — he soon will set his wrath on fire,
and, in his anger, thwart your enterprise!
O well for all who confidently fly to him!

PSALM 3

Trust in God, in the Midst of Enemies

I. The psalmist, assailed by enemies, cries to God for aid (2–4).
II. He has no fears, for the Lord is his support (5–7). III. He utters
his prayer with all confidence (8, 9).

1 A psalm of David, when he fled from Absalom, his son.

I 2 How many, Lord, there are that harass me!
How many are assailing me!

3 Full many there are that say to me:
  "For him there is no help in God!"
4 But you, Lord, are my shield,
  my glory; for you lift my head.

II 5 To the Lord I cried with all my voice;
  He heard me on his holy mount.
6 Yes, down I lay and fell asleep,
  and I awoke! The Lord is my support!
7 I shall not fear ten thousand men
  who round me stand in serried ranks to injure me.

III 8 Now rise, O Lord!
  My God, save me!
  You struck the jaws of all my foes,
  And broke the sinners' teeth.
9 Salvation is the Lord's own gift.
  O may your blessing rest upon your race!

PSALM 4

Trust in God, in the Midst of Unbelieving Sinners

I. The psalmist turns to God for help (2). II. He urges his foes to
refrain from sin (3–6). III. To those among his own people who
are wavering, he asserts his confidence in God (7–9).
  Because of its fitness as an evening prayer, this psalm is included
in Compline for Sunday.

1 *To the choirmaster. For stringed instruments. A psalm of David.*

I 2 When I petition, hear me, God, support of my just cause!
  In my distress you granted me relief;
  O pity me and hear my prayer.

II 3 O to what purpose, nobles, are you gross of heart?
  Why do you cherish idle dreams? And why pursue the lie?
4 This know: for his holy one the Lord did wondrous things!
  The Lord will answer me when I petition him.
5 Then take alarm and sin no more;
  take thought and search your hearts
  in nightly vigils and — desist!

⁶ Come, offer fitting sacrifice;
trust in the Lord.

III ⁷ "O who will make us happy?" many ask.
Lord, let your beaming face shine down on us.
⁸ You filled my heart with keener joy
than when a man abounds in wheat and wine.
⁹ In peace, as soon as I lie down, at once I fall asleep;
for you alone, O Lord,
are the rock of my security.

PSALM 5

Morning Prayer of a Good Man in the Midst of Enemies

I. David, in his morning prayer, asks for a favorable hearing from God (2–4). II. He knows that God abhors evildoers (5–7). III. The psalmist asks for guidance (8, 9). IV. He beseeches God to chastise his enemies (10, 11). V. He asks him, further, to bring joy to all those who turn to him in confidence (12, 13).

¹ To the choirmaster. On flutes. A psalm of David.

I ² My words with open ear receive, O Lord,
and to my groan attend.
³ Now hearken to my pleading voice,
my king, my God!
⁴ For 'tis to you, O Lord, I make appeal:
at dawn you hear my voice;
at dawn I offer you my prayers — and wait.

II ⁵ For you are not a God to take delight in wickedness;
no vicious man is welcome in your house;
⁶ nor do the godless in your presence stand their ground.
You hate all bent on wicked deeds;
⁷ all liars you destroy.
The Lord abominates
the treacherous man who thirsts for blood.

4:8. The psalmist compares his joy with that which an abundant harvest brings to the husbandman.

III   8 But I — unbounded is your kindliness! —
      will come into your house,
      and at your holy shrine bow down
    9 in reverence to you, O Lord.
      Guide me to do what you demand — to spite my enemies!
      Smooth out your path that lies ahead of me.

IV 10 For on their lips there is no truth;
      their heart plans treacherous deeds;
      their gullet is a yawning sepulchre;
      their tongue they use for flattery.
   11 Chastise them, God;
      and thwarted be their purposes;
      discard them for their many crimes,
      because against you they rebel!

V   12 May all rejoice who fly to you in confidence;
      may they exult eternally.
      Protect, and be a joy to those
      who love your name.
   13 Aye, Lord, you ever bless the holy man,
      and with benevolence, as with a shield, you compass him.

PSALM 6

Prayer of a Man Chastised by God

I. The psalmist prays for relief from his distress (2–4). II. He asks God to spare him from death (5, 6). III. His grief seems endless (7, 8). IV. The Lord hears his pleading cry; David spurns his enemies (9–11).
    This is the first of the penitential psalms.

   1 *To the choirmaster. For stringed instruments. An octave lower.*
    A psalm of David.

I   2 No more rebuke me in your anger, Lord,
      and in your rage chastise me not.
   3 Lord, pity me, for waning is my strength;
      heal me, O Lord, for broken is my frame.

    5:10c. *yawning sepulchre*: from which proceeds corruption.

⁴ My spirits, too, are deeply troubled.
But you, O Lord, how long. . . ?

II ⁵ Return, O Lord, and save my life;
and in your mercy rescue me.
⁶ In death, not one remembers you;
among the dead, who praises you?

III ⁷ Worn out am I with moaning;
with weeping every night I drench my bed;
with tears I wet my couch.
⁸ My eye is dimmed with grief —
an old man's eye! — so many are my foes.

IV ⁹ Away from me, you evildoers, each and all;
the Lord has heard my tearful voice;
¹⁰ the Lord has heard my pleading cry;
the Lord accepts my prayer.
¹¹ Shame all my foes and utterly confuse them;
shame them and rout them speedily.

PSALM 7

An Appeal to God, the Judge, by One Falsely Accused

I. The psalmist prays for help against his enemies (2, 3). II. He
protests that he is innocent of the crimes of which they charge
him (4–6). III. He appeals to God as the supreme judge of the
world (7–10). IV. God's judgment is just, certain, and terrible
(11–14). V. Punishment of the wicked is the result of their evil
ways (15–18).

¹ A lamentation of David, which he sang to the Lord because of
Chus, the Benjaminite.

I ² O Lord, my God, to you I confidently fly!

6:6. Revelation had not yet made clear what was the lot of those who
died before the Redemption. The ancient Hebrews thought that external
worship of God was impossible in the abode of the dead.

Save me from all my persecutors and deliver me!

3 Else — someone, lionlike, will seize
and mangle me, with none about to help.

II 4 O Lord, my God, if I incurred this guilt,
if wrong defiles my hands,
5 if I brought evil on my friend —
I who have spared my foes that did me wrong! —
6 then let my foe pursue and capture me,
and tread me underfoot,
and fling my glory to the dust.

III 7 O rise, Lord, in your wrath;
bestir yourself to curb the madness of my foes;
and rise in my behalf to execute the judgment you decreed.
8 The assembled nations — bid them 'round you range,
and over them preside upon your lofty throne.
9 The Lord — he is the nations' judge:
O do me justice, Lord, for I am innocent;
my conduct is above reproach.
10 Then stop the malice of the wicked crowd; sustain a holy man,
you, just God, the searcher of mind and heart.

IV 11 A shield to me is God,
who saves the true of heart.
12 A just judge is God, in truth,
a God who threatens everyday.
13 If they do not repent, he whets his sword,
and bends and aims his bow;
14 death-dealing darts he holds in readiness for them;
he makes his arrows firebrands.

V 15 Wrong he conceives, and is with malice big:
alas, delusion he begets!
16 A pitfall he has dug — he dug it deep! —
but falls into the pit he made!
17 His malice will recoil on his own head;
on his own pate his violence will fall.
18 For me, I praise the Lord, for he is just,
and to the harp I sing the Most High's name!

Psalm 8

The Majesty of God; the Dignity of Man

I. The psalmist contrasts God's majesty with the littleness of man
(2–5). II. He cites the glory and power to which God has raised
man (6–9). The last verse (10) repeats the second verse.

¹ To the choirmaster. To the melody of the song "The Wine
   Presses." A psalm of David.

I   ² O Lord, our Lord, how wondrous is your name in all the earth!
      Above the firmament you have extolled your majesty!
   ³ From babes and infant lips you draw a fitting hymn to shame
         your foes,
      to curb the malice of your enemies.
   ⁴ When at your firmament I gaze — your fingers' work,
      at moon and stars, which you have poised in space —
   ⁵ ah, what is man, that you should think of him;
      ah, what is mortal man, that you should care for him!

II ⁶ A little less than angels you created him;
      with dignity and glory him you crowned!
   ⁷ You gave him sway o'er all your handiwork;
      all things you placed beneath his feet:
   ⁸ yes, sheep and oxen, each and all,
      as well as all the roving beasts;
   ⁹ the birds in the sky, the fish in the sea —
      whatever travels ocean's paths.
   ¹⁰ O Lord, our Lord, how wondrous is your name in all the earth!

Psalm 9

This psalm comprises the matter of two psalms in the Hebrew text.
The division in question is warranted by the diversity of thought
in the two parts. In the Latin and English versions, however, they
are regarded as two parts of one psalm.

The psalm belongs to a group which are called alphabetical psalms.
In psalms of this type, in the Hebrew text, each verse or group of
verses begins with consecutive letters of the Hebrew alphabet. There

is no strict logical sequence of ideas in these alphabetical psalms, though, frequently enough, some relationship of thought is evident between the verses. Examples of such alphabetical psalms are, in addition to this one, Psalms 24, 33, 36, 110, 118, 144.

PSALM 9A

Thanksgiving for Victory Over the Gentiles

I. The psalmist extols the Lord for defeating his enemies (2–4). II. He describes the utter destruction of the wicked nations (5–7). III. The Lord is a just judge and a refuge to the oppressed (8–11). IV. The poet invites all men to sing the praises of God (12, 13). V. He appeals to God for further deliverance (14, 15). VI. The slaughter of the enemies is described (16, 17). VII. Again, the psalmist asks God to judge and punish the Gentiles (18–21).

1 To the choirmaster. To the melody "Mut Labben." A psalm
   of David.

I   2 O let me hymn you, Lord, with all my heart,
     tell out your every wondrous deed.
  3 Rejoice will I, and leap for joy in you,
     and sing, to the harp, your name, Most High:
  4 my enemies have given way and fallen back;
     completely routed, they were driven from your sight.

II   5 You took into your hands my judgment and my cause, and
     sat upon your throne, just judge.
  6 The nations you rebuked, the wicked you destroyed;
     their name you blotted out eternally.
  7 The foes are vanquished, to eternal ruin doomed;
     their cities you destroyed; their memory is gone.

III   8 The Lord, however, thrones eternally;
     for he has firmly fixed his judgment seat.
  9 With justice will he judge the world,
     with fairness give the peoples their award.
  10 The Lord will be a refuge to the oppressed,
     in moments of distress a timely refuge.
  11 And those who know your name will trust in you;
     you do not, Lord, abandon those who look to you.

IV ¹² Hymn, to the harp, the Lord who dwells on Sion;
among the nations tell his deeds.
¹³ A blood avenger, he kept in mind the poor,
and he did not forget their cry.

V ¹⁴ Lord, pity me; see what distress I suffer from my foes:
you ever snatch me from the gates of death,
¹⁵ that I may publish all your praises at the gates of Sion's citizens,
and glory in your help.

VI ¹⁶ Sunk are the nations in the pit they dug,
and, in the secret snare they laid, their foot is caught.
¹⁷ The Lord has shown himself, has justice done;
the sinner is ensnared in traps his own hands made!

VII ¹⁸ Away with sinners to the shades below,
with nations that forget their God!
¹⁹ The poor shall not forever fade from memory;
nor shall the hope of suffering men eternally be cast aside.
²⁰ Rise, Lord; let not man prevail;
and judge the nations ranged before your judgment seat.
²¹ Strike terror into them, O Lord;
and let the nations feel they are but men.

PSALM 9B

Against Oppressors of the People

The enemies referred to in this psalm are wealthy oppressors of the faithful. They are not foes from without; they are found among the psalmist's own people.
I. The psalmist expostulates with God for his seeming neglect of his afflicted people (1, 2). II. He describes the misconduct of these traitors, their temerity, their ruthless characters and conduct, their infidelity (3–11). III. He confidently appeals to the all-knowing and just God for help (12–15). IV. Certain that he will be heard, he celebrates his victory over these forces of evil (16–18).

I ¹ Why do you stand aloof, O Lord?
Why hide yourself in times of need?
² The sinner, meanwhile, domineers, the wretched man is vexed
and caught in traps the other has contrived!

II 3 Indeed, the sinner glories in his greed;
the grasping man blasphemes and spurns the Lord.
    4 And in his pride the impious man declares: "No question of
        revenge!
There is no God!" Such is the sum of his philosophy!
    5 Ever are his enterprises prosperous;
your judgments never occupy his thoughts;
for all his foes he feels contempt.
    6 And in his heart he says: "I shall not fail!
Long as I live, unhappy shall I never be!"
    7 His mouth is full of curses, fraud, and guile;
beneath his tongue mischief and trouble lurk;
    8 he sits in ambush near the villages;
in hidden nooks he slays the innocent;
his eyes spy on the needy man;
    9 he lurks in holes just like a lion;
he lies in wait to grasp the wretched man:
the wretched one he grasps and forces him into his net;
    10 he crouches, throws himself upon the ground:
the poor fall victims to his violence!
    11 And in his heart he says: "Oh, God forgets!
He turns his face away! He never looks!"

II 12 Then rise, Lord God; lift up your hand!
Do not forget the poor!
    13 Why does the godless man spurn God?
Why does he think: "No question of revenge"?
    14 But you have eyes: you notice toil and pain,
that you may take them in your hands.
To you the needy man commits himself;
the orphan is your ward.
    15 Then crush the might of spiteful, sinful man;
avenge his malice; let no trace of it remain.

V 16 The Lord is king eternally:
gone are the Gentiles from his land!
    17 You heard, O Lord, the yearning of the poor;
you lent your ear: you heartened them!
    18 O give the orphaned and oppressed their due award;
and let no mortal man spread terror any more.

Psalm 10

A Good Man's Stanch Confidence in God

I. The psalmist's enemies lay snares for him; fainthearted friends exhort him to seek refuge in the mountains (1–3). II. David rejects the advice. His faith in God, the just judge, is imperturbed (4–7).

¹ To the choirmaster. A psalm of David.

I   'Tis to the Lord I confidently fly! How can you say to me:
"Take wing! Off to the mountain like a bird!
² You see: the sinners bend their bow,
and place their arrow on the string,
to shoot in darkness at the true of heart.
³ When once the world is rocked to its foundations,
what can the good man do?"

II ⁴ The Lord is in his holy shrine;
the Lord — in heaven is his throne!
His eyes look down;
his glances test the humankind.
⁵ The Lord tests good and bad alike:
the man who loves iniquity he hates with all his heart.
⁶ He rains on sinners burning coals and brimstone;
"A scorching heat!" — such is the cup he offers them!
⁷ Indeed, the Lord is just, and justice wins his love;
the true of heart shall look upon his face.

Psalm 11

Against Proud and Treacherous Enemies

I. David laments the lack of truthfulness in his enemies (2, 3).
II. He asks God to silence their boasting, guileful tongues (4, 5).
III. God's response (6). IV. David reaffirms his confidence (7–9).

¹ To the choirmaster. An octave lower. A psalm of David.

I   2 Help, Lord! For pious souls are disappearing;
       fidelity has vanished from the race of men;
    3 falsehood pervades men's daily intercourse;
       their guileful lips reveal duplicity!

II 4 O may the Lord root out all guileful lips,
       the boastful tongue,
    5 the men who say: "Great things we compass with our tongue!
       Our lips are ours! Who, then, is master over us!"

II 6 "The lowly are afflicted; poor men groan;
       and therefore," says the Lord, "I now bestir myself!
       I will bestow the help each man desires!"

V   7 The Lord's words are sincere —
       as tested silver, purged from dross, and seven times refined.
    8 You, Lord, will rescue us,
       and screen us from this brood forevermore.
    9 The godless strut about us everywhere;
       the scum of men assume a domineering air!

PSALM 12

The Psalmist's Trust in God

**I. David grieves because God has forgotten him; he asks God to
help him once again (2–4). II. Without God's aid, his enemies
will gloat over his defeat. He puts all his trust in God's mercy (5, 6).**

     1 *To the choirmaster. A psalm of David.*

I   2 How long, O Lord? Will you forget me utterly?
        How long will you conceal your face from me?
     3 How long must I nurse sorrow in my soul,
        how long nurse grief within my heart from day to day?
     4 How long shall foe of mine still have the upper hand?
        Look down, and hear me, Lord, my God!

II   5 Enlight my eyes, or I shall fall asleep in death!
        Let not my enemy say: "I have defeated him!"
     6 Let not my foes boast of my fall;

for in your mercy I put all my trust.
O let my heart boast of your help;
I wish to hymn the Lord who has been good to me.

Psalm 13

The World's Corruption; Its Punishment

I. The psalmist deplores the widespread corruption he sees in the world. There are those who deny God's existence. Nevertheless, they cannot escape his all-seeing eye (1–3). II. These wicked men will one day realize their folly (4–6). III. For Israel, the psalmist seeks God's blessing (7).

¹ To the choirmaster. A psalm of David.

I   The fool says in his heart:
"There is no God!"
The world's corrupt! And shocking are its ways!
Not one there is that lives aright!
² From heaven the Lord looks forth upon the human race
to find one wise enough to search for God:
³ they all have strayed; all are corrupt;
not one there is that lives aright — not one!

II   ⁴ Will not the wicked world return to sanity?
They eat my people up as they eat bread!
The Lord they worship not.
⁵ In time they will be seized with panic fear,
for God is on the side of holy men.
⁶ You wish to foil the aspirations of the poor?
But mind: their refuge is the Lord!

III ⁷ May Israel's salvation come from Sion hill!
When once the Lord has veered the fortunes of his race,
then Jacob will exult; then Israel leap with joy!

───────────

13:4b. The line means: "They utterly destroy my people." Cf. Ps. 26:2.

PSALM 14

Who Dares Appear Before the Lord?

I. Who is worthy of dwelling in the presence of the Lord (1)?
II. The psalmist's reply: no one but the man of irreproachable
character (2–5). III. Such a man will always be happy (6).

¹ A psalm of David.

I   Who dares, O Lord, to linger in your tent,
or who to dwell upon your holy mount?

II   ² He who lives without reproach and gives to each his due,
whose norm of thinking is the truth,
³ whose tongue does not calumniate;
who does no evil to his fellow man,
nor on his neighbor heaps reproach;
⁴ who holds the wicked in contempt,
but honors those who fear the Lord;
⁵ who keeps his oath although it harms himself,
who lends no money out at usury,
and takes no bribe to harm the innocent.

III   ⁶ He who observes these rules
will be secure eternally.

PSALM 15

God, Our Greatest Good; the Source of
Resurrection and Eternal Life

I. The psalmist, repelled by the idolatry he sees about him, proclaims
his faith in God (1–6). II. He feels that the fellowship he now
enjoys with God will not be broken by death. He will participate
in the resurrection and eternal life (7–11).

¹ A miktam of David.

15:1. miktam: a musical term, the meaning of which is obscure. It has
been suggested that it means a poem of epigrammatic character.

I   Preserve me, God; I confidently turn to you;
2   to the Lord I say: "My Lord you are;
without you I have nothing that is good."
3   How wondrous is the love he poured into my heart
for all the saints that sojourn in his land!
4   All those that follow alien gods
heap grief on grief upon themselves.
I will not taste their sacrificial blood,
nor will my lips pronounce their names.
5   The Lord is my inheritance! He fills my cup!
My lot is in your hands.
6   A pleasant portion has been measured out to me;
my heritage is my supreme delight.

II   7   I bless the Lord, because he taught me how to choose:
both day and night my mentor is my heart.
8   I always keep the Lord before my eyes,
and on my right is he; I shall stand firm!
9   Therefore my heart is glad, my soul exults;
and so my body, too, will rest secure:
10   you will not leave my soul among the dead,
nor let your holy servant taste decay.
11   You will point out to me the way of life —
the plenitude of pleasures close to you;
aye, bliss at your right hand for all eternity!

PSALM 16

A Plea for Help Against Powerful Foes

I. The psalmist asserts that he is without fault in the service of God (1–5). II. He turns to God for help against his enemies (6–9a). III. Their attacks are violent (9b–12). IV. Again, he asks for God's judgment on his enemies. They are godless men. They

15:3b. *saints:* here, and in other psalms, means those men who are devoted, faithful worshipers of God.

15:10. The line means: "you will not permit my soul to be the eternal victim or prey of the dead."

think only of worldly values. The psalmist is confident that he will
ultimately see God face to face (13–15).

1 A prayer of David.

I   Hear, Lord, a just defence;
      hearken to my cry;
      lend ear to what I say: there is no guile upon my lips.
2 From your tribunal let my judgment come to me:
      your eyes see what is right.
3 O search my heart; a visit pay by night; try me by fire:
      you will not find iniquity in me.
      My lips have not transgressed,
4 as is the wont of men;
      I kept the letter of the law which your own lips have made;
5 my steps clung firmly to your paths;
      there was no faltering in my feet.

II 6 I call on you, for you will hear me, God;
      incline your ear to me and hear my plea.
7 O of your mercy give a wondrous proof:
      you rescue from their foes all those who fly to your right hand.
8 Protect me as the apple of your eye;
      beneath the shadow of your wings hide me
9 from sinners who do violence to me.

III   My foes swarm round me in a furious rage;
10 their callous heart they fasten tight;
      and they indulge in haughty speech.
11 They move about me now, and strain
      their eyes to throw me to the ground,
12 like a lion eager for its prey,
      like to a lion's cub that lurks in hidden places.

IV 13 Rise, Lord; confront him, hurl him down,
      and from the sinner save me with your sword;
14 with your own hand save me from men, O Lord,
      from men whose portion is this life,
      and whom you fatten with your wealth.
      Their children cloy themselves
      and to their children leave the residue.

¹⁵ For me, I shall be upright and behold your face;
for, when I wake to life, your sight will be my bliss.

PSALM 17

David Thanks God for Saving Him

The psalm has two parts. A. In the first part (2–31) there is a general description of how God intervened to help the psalmist. I. He thanks God for his help (2–4). II. He describes the dangers which had surrounded him (5–7). III. The terrifying phenomena of nature are an expression of God's anger (8–16). IV. The psalmist declares that he was saved because of his own irreproachable conduct (21–31). B. In the second part (32–46) the same thought continues, with a description of the particular blessings God had given the psalmist. I. God showed him how to do battle (32–35). II. He gave him powerful assistance (36–39). III. He put his enemies to flight (40–43). IV. David he made king of all peoples (44–46). In the epilogue, C, the psalm ends in a song of praise (47–51).

¹ *To the choirmaster. A psalm of David, the servant of the Lord,*
who spoke the words of this song to the Lord, after God had
delivered him from the hand of Saul and the power of all
his foes.

² *Thus he spoke:*

A I   I love you, Lord, my strength,
³ O Lord, my rock, my fortress, my deliverer,
my God, the stronghold of my weal, my guard!
⁴ I call upon the Lord, the worshipful,
and from my foes I shall be safe.

II ⁵ Around me surged the floods of death,
and torrents, threatening ruin, frightened me;
⁶ the ropes of death were round me coiled,
the snares of death had caught my feet:
⁷ in my distress I called upon the Lord,
and to my God I cried;

16:15b. when I wake to life: i.e., after the sleep of death. A similar idea is expressed in Ps. 15.

and in his shrine he heard my voice;
my cries came to his ears.

III   8 The earth then quavered and was rocked;
the bases of the mountains rocked
and reeled, because he burnt with rage.

9 And from his nostrils smoke arose,
and from his mouth consuming fire —
as coals made hot by him.

10 The heavens he declined, and down he came,
a darkling cloud beneath his feet.

11 He rode upon a cherub, and he flew,
and he was borne upon the wings of wind.

12 He put on gloom as 'twere a shroud,
and, as a covering, dark water and dense clouds.

13 And from the brightness in his countenance
coals were kindled into flame.

14 And the Lord thundered in the sky;
the Most High God sent forth his voice.

15 He let his arrows fly, flash after flash,
and scattered them, and routed them.

16 And then the bottom of the main appeared,
and bare were laid the bases of the world
upon the Lord's rebuke
and by the blast of his fierce wrath.

17 Down from on high, he reached his hand and caught me up,
and out he drew me from the rolling sea.

18 He set me free from my most valiant foe,
from those who hated me, who were more strong than I.

19 They rushed at me — an unblest hour for me! —
but then the Lord became my guard!

20 He led me out into a spacious field,
and, since he loves me, made me safe.

IV   21 The Lord requited me according to my faithfulness,
rewarded me because my hands are clean.

17:8–16. The intervention of God is splendidly described in metaphors taken from earthquake (8, 16) and storm (9–15). Similar descriptions are found in Psalms 28 and 96.

17:11. The cherubim carry the throne of God. Hence, he is said to "ride upon a cherub." Cf. Ps. 79:2; Ps. 98:1.

22   Yes, I was loyal to the Lord's commands,
     nor did I sin, revolting from my God.
23   All his decrees have been my guiding star,
     nor did I put his precepts out of sight.
24   Without a blame I was in serving him,
     and kept myself from guilt.
25   The Lord requited me according to my faithfulness;
     his eyes are witness that my hands are clean.
26   Your ways are kind in dealing with the kind,
     without a blame in dealing with a blameless man;
27   candid you are in dealing with a candid soul;
     but you act shrewdly with a crafty man.
28   Indeed, you save all humble folk,
     but you afflict the haughty eye.
29   For you, Lord, make my lamp to shine;
     my God, you turn my darkness into light.
30   Yes, with your help I rush on hostile bands;
     with my God's help I overleap a wall.
31   God's way is irreproachable;
     the Lord's word stands the test of fire.
     He is a shield to all who confidently fly to him.

B I 32 Who but the Lord is God?
         Who but our God is an impregnable rock? —
     33 the God who girdled me with fortitude
         and made my conduct irreproachable;
     34 who sped my feet as the feet of a deer,
         and safely placed me on a lofty crag.
     35 My hands he trained to fight,
         my arms, to bend the brazen bow.

   II 36 You handed me your shield that saves;
           your right hand bore me up;
           and your solicitude has made me great.
       37 Wide have you made the way for me to tread;
           my feet have not been faltering.
       38 I followed up my foes and captured them,
           nor did I turn till I was done with them.
       39 I crushed them utterly; they could not rise;
           they fell beneath my feet.

III ⁴⁰ You girdled me with fortitude to fight,
    you felled beneath my blows all that resisted me;
    ⁴¹ you put to rout my foes,
    and scattered all my enemies.
    ⁴² They cried — and none there was to help,
    cried to the Lord — he did not answer them.
    ⁴³ I scattered them like dust before the wind;
    like mud of the streets I trampled them.

IV ⁴⁴ You rescued me from mobbish turbulence;
    head of the Gentiles you appointed me.
    A tribe I did not know became my thrall;
    ⁴⁵ they heard my orders, and at once obeyed.
    Yes, foreigners have flattered me;
    ⁴⁶ foreigners grew pale, and trembling from their castles came.

C   ⁴⁷ Long live the Lord; blest be my rock;
    and God, my savior, be extolled —
    ⁴⁸ the God who put revenge into my hands.
    and made the nations subject to my will.
    ⁴⁹ You freed me from my enemies
    and made me triumph over all resisting me.
    You saved me from a violent man.
    ⁵⁰ Therefore, among the nations will I praise you, Lord,
    and sing a song in honor of your name.
    ⁵¹ You granted to your king great victories,
    and mercifully treated your anointed one —
    David and his eternal line.

Psalm 18

Praise of God, the Creator and Lawgiver

The psalm praises God as the author of all things, both in nature
and in the moral order. A. The first part (2–7) shows all nature
hymning the glory of God. I. The starry heavens and the firmament

---

17:44. Both domestic and foreign enemies have been overcome.
17:45b. *foreigners have flattered me:* i.e., they declare themselves subject
to me, even though they do so unwillingly and only through force.
17:51b. *your anointed one:* i.e., David, the King.

sing his praises (2–5b). II. The sun, in his daily course, honors him (5c, 7). B. The second part (8–15) honors God, the lawgiver. I. His law is in all ways perfect (8–11). II. The psalmist wishes to serve God, the creator and lawgiver, with constant observance of his precepts (12–15).

1 *To the choirmaster. A psalm of David.*

A I 2 The heavens tell the glory of God;
the firmament proclaims his craftsmanship:
3 as day to day pours out its utterance,
so night to night hands down intelligence!
4 Nor is the utterance made, nor the intelligence conveyed,
in accents not distinctly heard:
5 to every land their sound goes forth —
their message — to the world's last edge.

II And there he established a pavilion for the sun,
6 from which it sallies forth, as groom from bridal room,
and, like a giant, exults to run its course:
7 from heaven's marge it issues forth
and makes the round as far as heaven's verge;
and nothing is withdrawn from its warm glow.

B I 8 The law of the Lord is perfect — how it feasts the soul!
The ruling of the Lord is firm — how it instructs the ignorant!
9 The precepts of the Lord are right — how they delight the heart!
The Lord's command is clear — how it enlights the eye!
10 The worship of the Lord is pure — and it abides eternally!
The judgments of the Lord are true — and, each and all, are just!
11 And more desirable are they than hoard of precious gold,
and sweeter far than honeycomb and honey!

II 12 Your servant is attentive to them all,
in keeping them extremely diligent;
13 yet of his slips who is aware?
Cleanse me from faults not known to me!

18:4, 5. The voice of the heavens is clear and heard throughout the whole universe.

18:5c. *And there:* i.e., in the heavens.

18:12, 13. Even a good man, who is careful to observe the law, often, inadvertently, violates it; the psalmist prays that he may be cleansed from those sins of which he may be unconscious.

14 From pride, too, hold your servant back —
O may it never master me!
Then shall I be immaculate
and free from grave misdeed!
15 May all my spoken words and deepest thoughts
please you, O Lord, my savior and my rock!

PSALM 19

Prayer for the King as He Goes to War

I. The people ask God to give the king victory in the battle (2–6).
II. The psalmist has superb faith in God. He will not fail the king.
Upon God alone the victory depends (7–9). In the epilogue, the
Israelites again chant their prayer for David (10).

1 To the choirmaster. A psalm of David.

I 2 The Lord hear you in time of sore distress;
the name of Jacob's God be your defence!
3 May he send aid to you from out the shrine,
and out of Sion lend support to you!
4 May he remember all your offerings,
look kindly on your holocaust!
5 May he grant you your heart's desire,
and to fruition bring your every plan!
6 May we be gladdened by your victory,
and raise our banners in our God's name!
The Lord grant every prayer of yours!

I 7 By now, I know, the Lord has granted victory to his anointed one,
and from his holy heaven heard his prayer:
his strong right arm has been victorious.
8 Some trust in chariots, some in steeds:
but strong are we in the name of the Lord, our God.
9 The others — wearied and fallen, they! —
we stand and hold our ground.

10 O Lord, grant victory to the king!
And hear us on the day we call on you.

Psalm 20

God's Manifold Blessings to David; the Israelites' Gratitude

I. God has granted to David every desire of his heart (2–8).
II. The Israelites address their king. They seek for him lasting victory over his foes (9–14).

1 *To the choirmaster. A psalm of David.*

I 2 O Lord, the king rejoices in your might;
    because you helped, how jubilant is he!
  3 His heart's desire you granted him;
    the prayer upon his lips you did not spurn.
  4 His wish for happy blessings — you exceeded it,
    and on his head you placed a crown of purest gold.
  5 'Twas life he asked of you: you gave him
    length of days for endless time!
  6 Great is his glory, thanks to your help!
    High rank and splendor you conferred on him!
  7 You made him blest forevermore,
    entranced him by your gracious smile.
  8 Indeed, the king trusts in the Lord;
    and firm he will stand by the Most High's grace.

II 9 O may your hand bear down on all your foes,
    and may your right hand find your enemies!
  10 Consign them to a fiery furnace
    soon as your face will show itself.
    The Lord consume them in his wrath;
    may fire devour them all.
  11 Uproot their offspring from the land,
    their children from the human race.
  12 If they hatch plots to outrage you,
    if they lay snares, they never shall prevail.

20:5b. *length of days for endless time:* this is hyperbole, as used in the customary formula of salutation: "The king, may he live forever!" (Cf. 3 Kings 1:31.)

¹³ No, you will put them to the rout,
or aim your bow straight at their face.
¹⁴ Rise, Lord, with all your might,
and we will sing and celebrate your strength!

PSALM 21

The Passion of the Messias and Its Fruit

A. In the first part, the psalmist describes the Passion of the Messias
(2–22). I. Here are mentioned the sufferings of his soul (2–12):
he grieves that he is abandoned by God, who was the hope and help
of his fathers (2–6), that he suffers opprobrium and the scorn of
men (7–11). Therefore, he calls upon God to aid him (12). II. The
sufferings of his body are listed: torments, thirst, the weakness caused
by approaching death, the piercing of his hands, the sport made of
his clothing (13–19). III. Again, he calls upon God for help (20–22).
B. In the second part are described the fruits of the Passion (23–32).
I. The people of Israel will thank God and praise him for their
redemption (23–27). II. All nations will adore the true God
(28–30b). III. The Messias himself will live on and proclaim the
glory of God (30c–32).
Christ, dying on the cross, applied this psalm to himself (Mt.
27:46). The description of the Passion and the salvation wrought
by it show that the words of the psalm have been fulfilled in Christ
alone. The whole of Catholic tradition maintains this.

¹ *To the choirmaster. A psalm of David.*

I ² My God, my God, O why do you abandon me!
You turn your back upon my prayers, my urgent cries!
³ My God, I cry the livelong day: you do not hear;
at night: you lend no ear to me!
⁴ And yet, you dwell within the holy place,
O pride of Israel!
⁵ In you our fathers hoped;
they hoped, and you delivered them.
⁶ They cried to you, and they were saved;
they hoped in you, and were not put to shame.
⁷ But I — a worm I am and not a man;
the scorn of men, the people's laughingstock!
⁸ All those that see me laugh at me;

they grin and shake their heads:

9 "His trust is in the Lord: let him deliver him!
If he loves him, let him rescue him!"

10 Aye, you drew me forth from mother's womb,
made me secure at mother's breast.

11 To you I was entrusted at my birth,
and from my mother's womb my God are you!

12 Then do not stand aloof from me; I am in need;
draw near; for there is none to help.

II 13 Around me many bullocks stand;
the bulls of Basan ring me round.

14 With open jaws they threaten me,
like roaring lions bent on prey.

15 Like water that is spilt I am,
and out of joint are all my bones.
My heart is like a lump of wax:
it melts within my breast.

16 Like baking clay, my throat is parched;
my tongue cleaves to my jaws.
Into the dust you dragged me like a corpse.

17 Aye, many dogs encompass me;
a horde of evildoers rings me round.
They pierced my hands and feet;

18 count o'er I can my bones, one after one,
while they look on and at my sight rejoice.

19 My garments they divide among themselves,
and for my coat they cast the lot.

III 20 But you, O Lord, O do not stand aloof;
my help, make haste to bring me aid.

21 Preserve me from the sword,
and from the power of the dog;

22 save me from lions' jaws —
yes, me, the wretch, from the horns of oxen.

B I 23 I will proclaim your name to all my kin,
in full assembly give you praise.

24 "All you who fear the Lord give praise to him;

21:13b. *Basan*: this was a very fertile region, abounding in pasture lands. It was noted for the production of unusually fine cattle.

acclaim him, Jacob's children each and all.
25 For he did not disdain or spurn the wretch's wretchedness,
   or hide his face from him;
   and, when he called, he answered him."
26 You are my theme for praise when all the people meet;
   and in the presence of his servants will I pay my vows.
27 The poor shall eat their fill;
   and all that seek the Lord shall give him praise:
   "O may your hearts have life eternally!"

II 28 And all the confines of the earth,
   recalling this, will be converted to the Lord;
   and all the Gentile races
   will in his presence bend the knee.
29 For to the Lord belongs all royalty;
   among the Gentiles he holds sway.
30 And him alone the sleepers in the earth will, each and all, adore;
   to him all who go down to dust must bend the knee.

III   I, too, with heart and soul, will live for him.
31 Him shall my children serve;
32 to coming generations they will tell about the Lord:
   "This is what the Lord has done!"

Psalm 22

The Lord Is My Shepherd

I. The Lord provides me with food and drink; he protects me and directs me (1–4). II. He prepares for me an abundant table, and welcomes me into his house (5–6).

1 A *psalm of David.*

I   The Lord is my shepherd, and nothing do I want:
2 he bids me to repose in verdant pastures;
   to springs where I may rest he leads me on,
3 and there refreshes me.

22:1. In the Old and New Testaments, the image of God pasturing his people is very frequent; Christ applied the name "Good Shepherd" to himself.

He leads me onward over safe, straight paths
to manifest his holy name.
4 And should I cross a gloomy vale,
no evil shall I fear, because you are with me.
Your crook and staff —
they comfort me.

II 5 You spread for me a feast
for all my foes to see;
and you anoint my head with oil;
my cup is full up to the brim.
6 Kindness and grace will wait on me
through all the days of my life;
and I shall dwell in the house of the Lord
forever and evermore.

PSALM 23

Solemn Entry of the Lord Into His Holy Place

I. It is the Creator and Lord of the world who enters the holy place (1, 2). II. Those who would approach close to him must have innocence of life (3–6). III. The solemn entry of the Lord of hosts into his holy place (7–10).
    This psalm may have been composed by David when the Ark was first brought to Mount Sion; the psalm was chanted by many choristers.

1 A *psalm of David.*

I   The Lord's is the earth and all that fills it,
the globe and all that dwell on it.
2 For he it was that founded it upon the seas,
that placed it firmly on the streams.

II 3 Who shall ascend the mountain of the Lord,
or who stand in his holy place?

22:4c. The shepherd directed the flock with the crook, and defended them with the staff.
22:5b. His enemies will look on this favor enviously, but they will not be able to harm the psalmist.
23:2–3. The land rising out of the water is conceived as resting upon it. Cf. Ps. 135:6.

4 The innocent of hand and pure of heart,
who do not fix their minds on vanities,
or falsely swear to fellow men.

5 They shall receive a blessing from the Lord,
and a reward from God their savior.

6 Such are the kind of men that look for him,
that long to see the face of Jacob's God.

III   7 Lift up your heads, O gates;
O ancient portals, rise and open wide.
A glorious king is ready to go in.

8 "Who is this glorious King?"
"The strong and mighty Lord;
the Lord, a mighty warrior."

9 Lift up your heads, O gates;
O ancient portals, rise and open wide.

10 "Who is this glorious king?"
"The Lord of hosts: he is the glorious king."

PSALM 24

Petition for Forgiveness and Freedom
From All Troubles

The psalm is alphabetical (cf. Introduction, Ps. 9). I (1–7) and
III (16–22) are prayers. II. This is a meditation on the goodness of
God toward the righteous (8–15). The psalmist asks of God forgiveness for his sins (7–11, 18) and begs that he might have the
grace to live according to God's precepts (4, 5; cf. 8–10, 12), and
he asks for deliverance from his afflictions (17, 18, 20) and for
protection from his enemies (2, 19; cf. 15).

1 A psalm of David.

I   To you I lift my soul,
O Lord, my God!

2 In you I trust: do not discomfort me!
Let not my enemies triumph over me.

23:7. The gates are hardly high enough for so great a God (symbolically
present over the Ark) to pass through; they should raise their *heads,* i.e.,
their upper portions.

3 No one that ever hopes in you is put to shame;
those will be shamed who lightly break their faith.
4 O Lord, make known your ways to me;
and teach me all your paths;
5 O guide me to obey your true demands;
teach me; you are my Savior God.
In you I always trust.
6 Recall your mercies, Lord,
your kindnesses from immemorial time.
7 Do not recall my youthful sins, my faults.
According to your mercy, Lord,
according to your kindness,
do, pray, give thought to me.

II   8 Good and holy is the Lord;
he therefore shows the way to sinful men.
9 He guides the humble by his just demands,
and to the humble shows his way.
10 The Lord's ways are all kindness and fidelity
to such as keep his precepts and his covenant.
11 In honor of your name, O Lord,
forgive my sin; for it is great.
12 Where is the man that fears the Lord?
He teaches him which way to choose.
13 In happiness he will himself abide;
his children will possess the land.
14 A friend to such as fear him is the Lord;
he manifests his covenant to them.
15 My eyes are ever straining toward the Lord;
for he will draw my feet from out the snare.

III 16 O look upon me; pity me!
For I am wretched and forlorn.
17 Relieve the anguish of my soul,
and rescue me from my anxieties.
18 O see my trouble and my misery;
and pardon all my sins.
19 Look at my foes! How numerous they are!
They hate me in their deepest soul.
20 O save my life and rescue me.

Do not discomfit me; I flee to you for help.
21 May uprightness and innocence e'er be my shield;
because I put my trust in you, O Lord.
22 Deliver Israel, O God,
from all its straits!

PSALM 25

The Psalmist, Falsely Accused, Turns to God for Judgment

I. David protests his innocence. He calls upon God to judge him (1, 2). II. He lays open to God his mode of life: he is constant in God's service, he is zealous in extending the worship of God, he has no dealings with evil men (3–8). III. The psalmist asks that he will not be condemned along with evil men (9–12).

The priest recites vv. 6–12 at the *Lavabo* of the Mass.

1 A *psalm of David.*

I   O do me justice, Lord: I walk the ways of innocence,
and, trusting in the Lord, I have not swerved.
2 Test me, O Lord, and scrutinize my acts;
O search my heart, my inmost soul.

II   3 Your kindness is my guiding star;
I walk the ways your truth points out.
4 I do not mix with wicked men,
or join a crowd of guileful ones.
5 I hate all evildoers' company,
and mingle not with godless men.
6 I wash my hands among the innocent
and join the throng about your altar, Lord,
7 to sing your praises loud and clear
and tell out all your wondrous deeds.
8 O Lord, I love the house in which you dwell,
the place in which your glory is enshrined.

III   9 Do not destroy my life along with sinful men,
or put an end to me with men that thirst for blood,
10 whose hands are steeped in crime,
whose palms are filled with bribes.

11 But I — I walk the ways of innocence;
have mercy, you, on me; deliver me.

12 My foot is firmly planted on an even path;
in the assemblies will I bless the Lord.

PSALM 26

Undaunted Trust in God

A. I. The psalmist asserts his unconquered trust in God, the light
of his life (1–3). II. He knows that in the temple, where he will be
united with him, he will be safe from his enemies (4–6). B. I. He
pleads that he may not be abandoned by God (7–10). II. Confident he is that he will be led along a safe path, free from the
trickery of foes (11, 12); with stanch faith, he rouses himself to
even greater trustfulness (13, 14).

1 A *psalm of David.*

A I   The Lord is my salvation and my light: whom shall I fear?
The Lord protects my life: who, then shall frighten me away?

2 When evildoers rush on me to eat my flesh —
ill-wishers, one and all — they fall and grovel in the dust;

3 and should I face a hostile camp, my heart shall never fear;
if war against me looms, I still have confidence.

II 4 One thing I ask of the Lord, one I request:
to live in the house of the Lord all my life
to gaze upon the temple of the Lord
and taste his kindness to the full.

5 Within his tent he will conceal me in an evil hour,
and hide me in a secret corner of his tent.
He will uplift me to a lofty rock.

6 And now my head is raised
above the foes that ring me round;
and in my joy I offer sacrifices in his tent;
with voice and cymbal will I praise the Lord.

25:12. *on an even path:* i.e., one upon which I can walk with no danger
of falling.
26:2. Cf. Ps. 13, 4b.

B I ⁷ Hear, Lord, my pleading voice;
         take pity on me and answer me.
       ⁸ My heart speaks out to you; my eyes strain after you;
         your face, O Lord, I long to see.
       ⁹ Do not conceal your face from me;
         do not repel your servant angrily.
         You are my help: O do not cast me off!
         Do not abandon me, O God, my savior.
      ¹⁰ And should my father and my mother e'er abandon me,
         yet will the Lord be my support.

 II ¹¹ Teach me, O Lord, your way;
         escort me on an even path to spite my foes.
      ¹² Do not allow my foes to work their will on me,
         for my assailants are mendacious witnesses, men breathing
            violence.
      ¹³ I trust I shall yet see the Lord's good things
         here in the land of life.
      ¹⁴ Await the Lord, and act the man;
         be stout of heart; await the Lord.

PSALM 27

A Prayer of Supplication and Thanksgiving

I. The psalmist beseeches God to protect him from malicious enemies (1–5). II. So certain is he that he will be heard that he anticipates with thanksgiving the favor asked by him (6, 7). III. He prays for the welfare of the king and the people (8, 9).

       ¹ A psalm of David.

 I   To you, O Lord, I cry;
         my rock, do not be deaf to me;
         for if you do not answer me, I shall be like the men that sink
            into the pit.

26:11b. *on an even path:* cf. Ps. 25:12.
26:13b. *in the land of life:* i.e., before I die, I hope that I will experience the grace and favor of God.

² O hear my pleading voice when I appeal to you,
when toward your holy shrine I lift my hands.
³ O do not snatch me off along with sinful men,
with men determined to do wrong:
peace with their fellow men is on their lips,
but there is malice in their hearts.
⁴ Do unto them according to their deeds,
in just requital for their heinous crimes.
As they by others do, so do by them;
make their own deeds recoil on them.
⁵ They do not heed the dealings of the Lord or understand his
handiwork:
may he demolish them and never build them up again!

II ⁶ Blest be the Lord, for he has heard my pleading voice,
the Lord, my strength, my shield!
⁷ In him my heart has confidently hoped, and I found help;
therefore my heart exults, and with my song I give him praise.

III ⁸ Strength to his people is the Lord;
the safeguard of his weal to his anointed one.
⁹ Save you your people, Lord, and bless your heritage;
and shepherd them, and hold them in your arms eternally.

Psalm 28

The Majesty of God Seen in the Tempest

I. The psalmist urges the people to praise the might of God (1, 2).
II. God speaks through the tempest; his powerful voice, manifested
through the thunder, agitates the sea, the cedars of Lebanon and
Hermon, the desert of Cades, the trees, the wood (3–9). III. The
Lord, king from ancient times, now and forever, will bless his
people (10, 11).

¹ *A psalm of David.*

I   Acclaim the Lord, O sons of God;
acclaim the might and glory of the Lord!
² Acclaim the Lord for his glorious name;
in holy vesture robed, adore the Lord!

II   3 The voice of the Lord is on the waters, hark!
It thundered! It was God's majesty!
The Lord is on the boundless waves.

    4 The voice of the Lord — a voice of might!
The voice of the Lord — a voice of majesty!

    5 The voice of the Lord dismembers cedars;
the Lord dismembers the cedars of Lebanon,

    6 bids Lebanon leap as a bullock leaps,
and Sarion, as the young of the buffalo.

    7 The voice of the Lord calls forth the fiery flash;

    8 the voice of the Lord makes deserts reel;
the Lord makes the desert of Cades reel.

    9 The voice of the Lord twists oaks and strips the woods;
and in his temple rings the cry of "Glory!" from all lips.

III 10 The Lord throned on the flood;
the Lord will throne a king forevermore.

    11 The Lord will give his people fortitude:
the Lord will bless his people with peace.

PSALM 29

Thanksgiving for Deliverance From Death

The harpist renders praise to God (2). A. He is grateful that he
was preserved from death; short was his affliction; long-lasting is
God's goodness (3–6). B. He tells what his offense had been. I. He
had sinned by rash confidence (7, 8). II. But once again humble, he
turned to supplications (9–11). III. Now he makes thanksgiving
for the favor he has received (12, 13).

1 *A psalm of David. A hymn for the feast of the dedication of
the temple.*

2 My praise to you, O Lord! You have delivered me;
to my foes you have not given triumph over me.

28:6b. *Sarion:* the Phoenician name for Hermon.

28:8b. The desert of Cades is the region southeast of Palestine, near the
border of Edom. Cf. Num. 20:16 ff. The Israelites encamped there before
entering the Promised Land.

28:9. While the storm rages on earth, in heaven all sing the praises of God.

A   3 O Lord, my God;
       I cried to you; you gave me health.
     4 O Lord, you led me out of death's domain;
       you rescued me from those that sink into the pit.
     5 Make music to the Lord, O all his saints,
       and to his holy name give thanks.
     6 But for a moment lasts his wrath.
       and lifelong is his kindliness.
       Tears will come at eventide;
       at dawn comes jubilant joy.

B I   7 Alas, in my self-confidence I said:
       "Unhappy I shall never be!"
     8 It was your favor, Lord, that gave me pomp and state;
       you hid your face: gone was my peace of soul!

  II   9 To you, O Lord, I cry,
       and I implore the mercy of my God:
    10 "What will my death avail,
       what if I sink into the pit?
       Will dust give praise to you
       and blaze abroad your faithfulness?"
    11 Then hear, O Lord; be merciful to me;
       O be my helper, Lord!

 III 12 You turned my wailing into dancing joy,
       removed my sackcloth, and with gladness girt me round!
    13 Now let my soul, a never-silent harp, sing songs to you!
       O Lord, my God, my praise to you in all eternity!

Psalm 30

An Appeal in Time of Great Distress;
Thanksgiving for Answered Prayer

I. The psalmist, oppressed with troubles, turns to God with all
confidence (2–7), for God it was who had saved him on other
occasions (8, 9). II. Now, languishing in overwhelming difficulties,
he is laughed at by his enemies, forgotten by his friends; he is like

---

29:10. Cf. Ps. 6:6.

one dead (10–14), but not failing in trust, he puts himself in the hands of God (15–19). III. At once certain that his prayer has been heard, he hymns the goodness of God (20–23) and exhorts all good men to love God and be of courageous heart (24, 25).

The words of v. 6 were uttered by Christ as he was dying on the cross; the whole psalm describes the Passion of our Lord and his filial devotion to his Father.

1 *To the choirmaster. A psalm of David.*

I   2   To you, O Lord, I confidently fly: O may I never meet with shame!
Just you are: deliver me!
  3   Incline to me your ear;
make haste to rescue me.
A rock of refuge be to me,
a castle, fortified to rescue me.
  4   Indeed, you are my rock, my citadel;
in honor of your name, then, be my escort and my guide!
  5   O free me from the secret snare they laid for me.
You are my safe retreat!
  6   My spirit I commit into your hands;
deliver me, O Lord, my faithful God.
  7   All worshipers of idols you abominate:
but I trust in the Lord.
  8   I shall yet be enraptured by your tenderness:
for you looked kindly on my misery,
and helped me in my evil hour.
  9   You did not hand me over to my enemy,
but placed my feet on spacious ground.

II   10   Again, Lord, pity me; for I am in distress;
my eyes, my soul, my frame — all waste away.
  11   My life is wearing out with grief;
my years are one long sigh;
in my affliction wanes my strength,
and wasted are my bones.
  12   A byword to all foes am I,
to neighbors a reproach, to friends a fright.
They see me out of doors and run away from me.
  13   Effaced am I from memory, as good as dead,
I am like shattered earthenware.

14 Yes, yes, I heard the whisper of the crowd —
there's fright on every face!
Against me they conspire; they plot to take my life.

15 But I have confidence in you, O Lord;
I say: "You are my God!"

16 My fate is in your hand.
From foe, from persecutor: rescue me.

17 Smile on your servant once again,
and in your tenderness deliver me.

18 O do not shame me, Lord; I worship you.
But shame the godless; silence them; hurl them down into the pit.

19 Strike dumb all lying lips that heap abuse,
from proud contempt, upon a holy man.

III 20 How great your kindness, Lord,
reserved for those who worship you in fear!
How gracious, you, to those who confidently fly to you,
for all the world to see.

21 You shield them by your shielding glance
from men's conspiracy;
You hide them in your tent
from wrangling tongues.

22 Blest be the Lord: a wondrous proof of tenderness
he gave me in a city strongly fortified.

23 Yet I had thought in my bewilderment:
"Cut off I am — off from your kindly look."
But no: you heard my pleading voice
when I appealed to you.

24 O love the Lord, all you his saints;
the Lord preserves the faithful souls,
but punishes the proud abundantly
for all their deeds.

25 Be cheered and stout of heart,
all you that hope in the Lord.

PSALM 31

Happy the Man Whose Sin Has Been Pardoned

This is the second of the penitential psalms. I. In the introduction, the psalmist describes the happiness of a man whose sins have been remitted (1, 2). II. He tells what he had experienced: when he kept his sins to himself, he was tortured night and day; when he confessed them, he received pardon (3–5), and he advises all good men to seek God whenever they are in difficulties (6, 7). III. Now God speaks, warning men that they should not be like dumb beasts that lack all reason (8, 9). IV. In the epilogue, the psalmist proclaims that the source of all joy is hope in God (10, 11).

1 A *psalm of David.*

I   O well for him whose wrongs have been remitted,
whose sin has been removed from sight!
2 Well for the man to whom the Lord does not impute his guilt,
and in whose heart there is no guile.

II 3 I kept my secret, wasted were my bones
amidst my constant groans.
4 By day and night your hand weighed heavy on me,
and waning was my strength as if from summer heat.
5 My sin I did confess to you;
my guilt I did not hide.
I said: "I do confess unto the Lord my wrong!"
And you forgave the guilt contracted by my sin.
6 And therefore every pious soul will pray to you in time of sore distress.
A tidal wave may rush toward him:
to him it will not make its way.
7 You are my haven: from my straits you will deliver me,
and you will fill my soul with joy in my salvation.

III 8 "Now will I lesson you, show you the way to tread;
teach you I will, and fix my gaze upon you:
9 'O do not be like horse or mule that has no sense,
whose mood is tamed by bridle and by bit —
they come not near you otherwise!' "

IV ¹⁰ Full many are the pangs of godless men,
    but mercy shrouds the man that trusts the Lord!
  ¹¹ O holy souls, joy in the Lord exceedingly;
    hearts good and true, exult!

PSALM 32

Praise of the Power and Providence of God

I. The psalmist invites the faithful to praise the powerful, just,
and good God (1–5). II. By his mere word he created the earth
(6, 7). III. By it he governs the people (8–12). IV. With his
insight he knows all things (13–15). V. By his power he gives
victory and salvation (16–19). VI. In the epilogue, the psalmist
advises all men to put their trust in God (20–22).

I ¹ Be jubilant in the Lord, O holy souls;
    for rousing praise beseems the true of heart!
  ² O hymn the praises of the Lord upon the lyre:
    upon the ten-stringed harp make melody to him!
  ³ O sing to him a song not sung before!
    Sing well! Your singing rend the air!
  ⁴ The word of the Lord rings true,
    and all his works prove his fidelity.
  ⁵ The Lord loves what is right and just;
    and with his gracious acts the earth o'erflows.

II ⁶ A word of the Lord has made the firmament;
    a breath of his mouth, its starry hosts.
  ⁷ As in a bag he gathers up the waters of the main,
    and in their proper place confines the rolling waves.

III ⁸ May all the earth revere the Lord;
    may all the world's inhabitants fear him!
  ⁹ He spoke the word, and they were made;
    he uttered the command: they came to be!
  ¹⁰ The Lord frustrates the nations' plans;
    he thwarts the peoples' purposes.
  ¹¹ The planning of the Lord endures for aye;
    his kindly purposes, from age to age.

12 Well for the race whose God is the Lord,
    the people which he made his chosen heritage.

IV 13 From heaven the Lord looks down,
    and watches all mankind;
  14 and from his dwelling place he looks far out
    on all that dwell on earth:
  15 he formed the heart of every one of them;
    he keeps an eye on all their deeds.

V 16 No king prevails by mass of fighting men;
    no warrior is saved by dint of strength;
  17 no horse assures a victory;
    its bulk and strength will never save the day.
  18 Mark well: the eyes of the Lord are on his worshipers,
    on all that trust his grace,
  19 and thus he saves their lives from death,
    and feeds them in a time of dearth.

VI 20 We hopefully await the Lord;
    our help, our shield is he.
  21 In him, therefore, our heart delights,
    and in his holy name we trust.
  22 O may your mercy, Lord, descend on us,
    just as we hope in you.

PSALM 33

Fear of God and Its Reward

The psalm is alphabetical (cf. the introduction to Ps. 9). It has three parts. I. The psalmist calls upon his people to sing the praises of God (2–4). II. He refers (vv. 5, 7, 8, 11) to a great danger from which he was saved; hence, he concludes that God's goodness should always be trusted (5–11). III. In the last part, David shows that those who reverence God and observe his precepts enjoy happiness and a long life (12–23).

1 *A psalm of David, when he feigned madness before Abimelech,*
    with the result that Abimelech sent him away, and he escaped.

I 2 At all times I will bless the Lord,
    and ever be his praise upon my lips.

3 The Lord shall be my boast;
  let humble people hearken and rejoice!
4 Extol the Lord with me;
  in chorus let us glorify his name!

II 5 I sought the Lord; he answered me;
  from all my fears he rescued me.
6 Look up to him! Be cheered!
  Let not your faces blush with shame!
7 You see: a wretch cried out; the Lord heard him;
  from all his troubles he delivered him!
8 A camp the angel of the Lord erects
  about his worshipers, and thus delivers them.
9 O mark and taste the goodness of the Lord!
  Well for the man that confidently flies to him!
10 O fear the Lord, all you, his saints;
  no want befalls his worshipers.
11 Great men have been reduced to beggary and dearth;
  but those who seek the Lord lack nothing good.

III 12 Come, children, hear my voice,
  and I will lesson you in the fear of the Lord.
13 Where is the man in love with life,
  who longs for prosperous days?
14 Refrain your tongue from ill,
  your lips from treacherous words.
15 Shun what is bad, do what is good;
  seek after peace in thought and deed.
16 The eyes of the Lord look on the saints;
  his ears take notice of their cry.
17 The face of the Lord abhors all evil men;
  he blots their memory from the earth.
18 The saints cry out: the Lord hears them;
  from all their straits he rescues them.
19 The Lord is near to the crushed of heart;
  and broken spirits he restores.
20 A holy man has many ills to bear:
  from all the Lord delivers him:
21 he keeps from harm his every bone;
  not one of them is crushed.

22 To death a godless man is by his malice hurled;
and those who hate the good will come to grief.

23 The Lord preserves his servants' lives;
and he who flies to him will never come to grief.

PSALM 34

A Petition for Help Against Unjust and
Ungrateful Persecutors

I. The psalmist asks God to put his enemies to confusion (1–6).
II. He describes the persecution they have instigated against him
(7–12): they try to trick him; they accuse him unjustly. III. These
persecutors he once had befriended, but they show no gratitude
(13–16). IV. He beseeches the help of God more ardently (17–28):
he asks that God will no longer show patience toward these men
(17–21), nor be silent, nor be unheedful, as though he were asleep
(22–25); finally, that he will bring joy to him and all good men
(26–28).

1 A *psalm* of *David*.

I   Fight, Lord, with those who fight with me,
and combat those who combat me!

2 Take hold of shield and buckler,
and rise to bring me aid!

3 Brandish the spear, hold my pursuers back,
and say to me: "Your savior am I!"

4 Confound and shame all those that seek my life!
Away with those, in utter shame, who plan to do me harm!

5 Be they like chaff before the gust,
when the Lord's angel beats them back!

6 Their way be dark and slippery,
when the Lord's angel tracks them down!

II 7 For unprovoked they spread their net for me,
and unprovoked they dug a pit for me.

8 May ruin come upon them unexpectedly:
the net they spread be their own snare;
the pit they dug be their own grave.

9 For me, in the Lord I will exult;
and in his help I will rejoice.

¹⁰ With all my strength I will cry out:
"O Lord, who is your peer?
You save a wretch from one in power,
a poor and wretched man from robber's hand."
¹¹ Yes, violent men arose to testify;
for wrongs not known to me they held me to account.
¹² My kindness they repaid with evil deeds;
into gloom they plunged my soul.

III ¹³ And yet, when they were ill, I donned the sackcloth,
and chastised myself with fasts;
and prayed and prayed with all my heart.
¹⁴ As for friend or brother, so I went about disconsolate;
as one that mourns his mother, so I bowed my head in grief.
¹⁵ But when I tripped, they gathered in high glee;
they gathered for an unexpected stroke;
they mangled me unceasingly;
¹⁶ they harassed me; they mocked at me;
they gnashed their teeth and grinned.

IV ¹⁷ O Lord, how long will you look on?
From roaring beasts, from lions, rescue me.
¹⁸ Thanks will I give you where the people gather,
and praise when all the people meet.
¹⁹ Let not my foes unjustly gloat o'er me;
let not my enemies unfairly leer at me.
²⁰ They do not say what makes for peace;
'gainst peaceful citizens they plan their plots.
²¹ They open wide their mouths to mock at me;
they say: "Ha! Ha! We saw it with our eyes!"

²² You saw, O Lord; O do not fail to act;
Lord, do not stand aloof from me.
²³ Awake, and rise to my defense.
My God, my Lord, take up my cause.
²⁴ Since you are just, have justice done me, Lord;
my God, let them not gloat o'er me.
²⁵ Let them not think: "Ha! Ha! Just what we wanted!"

34:15c. They tore him to pieces, as wild beasts might their prey; or as
we might speak of tearing someone's reputation to pieces.

Let them not say: "We have completely ruined him!"
26 Let all together meet with utter shame
who gloat upon my misery;
let all put on the rags of shame
who wish to lord it over me.
27 Bid all who wish me well hold jubilee;
unending be their cry:
"The Lord be praised;
he has his servant's weal at heart!"
28 My theme, then, shall your justice be;
upon my lips shall never die your praise.

PSALM 35

On Human Wickedness and Divine Providence

The psalm deals with I: the heinousness of human depravity which,
forgetful of divine vengeance, shrinks from no wrong (2–5), and
II: the providence of God, which is the source of all security, joy,
and life (6–10). III. The psalmist asks this good God to give him
grace and to protect him against enemies (11–13).

1 *To the choirmaster. A psalm of David, the servant of the Lord.*

I 2 With wickedness the sinner's heart holds colloquy;
against the fear of God his eyes are shut.
3 Himself he flatters with the thought:
"My guilt is neither noticed nor abhorred!"
4 His words are sheer iniquity and guile;
he ceased to do and think the right.
5 He hatches wickedness upon his nightly couch;
bent on a wayward course, he does not shrink from what is base.

II 6 O Lord, your mercy reaches to the sky;
your faithfulness, up to the very clouds.
7 Your justice is like the hills of God;
your judgments, to the deepest main;
both man and beast you keep alive, O Lord.
8 How precious is your graciousness, O God!
Men flee for shelter 'neath the shadow of your wings;

35:3. The sinner builds up a false hope for himself that his sin will
neither be detected nor punished.

⁹ they feast upon the fatness of your house;
with torrents of your own delights you slake their thirst.
¹⁰ Indeed, in your possession is the fount of life,
and in your light we see the light.

III ¹¹ Keep in your grace your worshipers;
and keep your kindly disposition toward the true of heart.
¹² Let not the proud man's foot betrample me;
let not the sinner's might turn me adrift.
¹³ See how the wicked men have fallen to the ground:
thrown down they are and cannot rise!

PSALM 36

The Lot of Good Men and That of Evil Ones

This alphabetical psalm (cf. the introduction to Ps. 9) deals with the problem of retribution. The psalmist notes that good men are appalled when they see wicked people prospering and flourishing (1). His answer to the problem is that their prosperity does not last long and that the punishment which their sins deserve comes quickly upon them (2). This solution of the question is repeated throughout the psalm, either by showing that the wicked are punished (9, 10, 12–15, 16, 20, 21 f., 28, 35 f., 38) or by representing the good as happy and prosperous (3–7, 9–11, 16 f., 18 f., 21 f., 23–28, 29–34, 37, 39 f.).

¹ *A psalm of David.*

Be not provoked by evildoers' luck,
and do not envy any bent on wickedness.
² Like grass, they swiftly droop;
like green things in the field, they fade.
³ Trust in the Lord; do what is good:
long will you live on earth, lapped in security!
⁴ Find in the Lord your happiness,
and he will grant your heart's desire.
⁵ Trust to the Lord your whole life's course,
and hope in him: then he will act!

36:3b. *long will you live on earth,* i.e., in the promised land and enjoy its blessings (cf. vv. 9, 11, 22, 29, 34).

6 Your justice he will make like to a rising light;
your right, like to the noonday sun.

7 Repose upon the Lord,
and trust in him.
Be not provoked by any man's prosperity,
by anyone that hatches wicked schemes.

8 No, keep your temper; quell your rage;
be not provoked; or else you sin.

9 All sinners will be rooted out;
but all who hope in the Lord possess the land.

10 A little while — the wicked are no more;
look for their place — they are not there!

11 The gentle will possess the land,
and will enjoy a plenitude of peace.

12 The sinner hatches evil plots against the saint,
and grinds his teeth, enraged at him.

13 The Lord laughs him to scorn;
his day, he sees, is drawing near.

14 The godless draw their sword and bend the bow
to level the wretched beggar with the dust,
to kill the upright man;

15 yet will the sword pierce their own hearts;
their bows shall break.

16 The little that a good man has is better far
than all the heaped-up wealth of godless men.

17 The might of godless men shall come to nought;
the saint is borne up by the Lord.

18 The Lord takes care of good men's lives;
their heritage shall last eternally.

19 They are not humbled in adversity;
in days of dearth they have their fill.

20 The godless, on the contrary, shall perish;
the enemies of the Lord shall fade away like the bloom of
meadowlands;
like smoke they disappear.

21 The bad man borrows, and makes no return;
the good man has a heart, and freely gives.

22 Those whom he blesses shall possess the land;
those whom he curses are destroyed.

23 Man's steps are steadied by the Lord;
   he is delighted with his way of life:
24 he trips, yet is he not laid low;
   the Lord upholds him by the hand.
25 A child I was, and am an old man now;
   I never saw a good man yet left in the lurch,
   nor did I see his children begging bread.
26 He always has a heart and freely lends;
   his children shall be blessed.
27 Then turn away from evil, and do good;
   that thus you may remain secure eternally.
28 The Lord loves what is right,
   and ne'er deserts his saints.
   The bad shall be destroyed;
   their offspring shall be rooted up.
29 The good men shall possess the land,
   and shall forever dwell upon its soil.
30 The good man's lips speak words of wisdom;
   his tongue expresses what is right.
31 The law of the Lord reigns in his heart;
   his steps are never faltering.
32 The godless man spies on the good;
   he plots to take his life.
33 The Lord will not abandon him to that man's grip,
   nor yet condemn him on the judgment day.
34 Trust in the Lord;
   observe his law;
   and he will prosper your possession of the land.
   You will serenely see the downfall of the bad.
35 I saw a rascal riot in his pride,
   who like a branching cedar spread himself:
36 when I passed by, he was no more;
   I looked for him: he was not found!
37 Look at, and mark, the good and virtuous man:
   a peaceful man is sure of his posterity;
38 but all sinners will be rooted up;
   the godless men's posterity will be wiped out.
39 The welfare of the just is from the Lord;
   he is their refuge in the days of need;

40 yes, he, the Lord, helps and delivers them;
   he shields and rescues them from wicked men,
   because they confidently fly to him.

PSALM 37

Prayer of a Sinner Afflicted by God

I. The psalmist is suffering because of his sins; he asks that God be merciful to him (2–5). II. He describes his misery (6–13): stricken by a repulsive disease, he languishes away (6–9); he is abandoned by his friends and annoyed by enemies (10–13). III. He remains silent, putting his trust in God alone (14–17). IV. He again confesses his fault and turns to God for aid (18–23). This is the third of the penitential psalms.

1 A psalm of David. For a memorial.

I 2 Lord, do not chide me in your anger;
    nor yet chastise me in your rage.
  3 Alas, your shafts are stuck in me;
    your hand is bearing down on me.
  4 No health is in my flesh: so great your wrath;
    no soundness in my bones: so great my sin!
  5 A torrent of guilt is overwhelming me;
    a heavy load — it wears me down exceedingly.

II 6 Yes, foul and rankling are my sores:
    my folly was the cause of these!
  7 Quite bowed and stooped I am;
    the livelong day I walk about disconsolate.
  8 My loins are one great festering sore;
    no healthy spot is in my flesh.
  9 I languish: I am completely broken down;
    I groan — I am so sore at heart!
  10 Well-known to you is all my longing, Lord;
    my sigh does not escape your ears.
  11 My heart's athrob; my strength is gone;
    the light of my eyes itself is failing me.

37:6–13. This description of sickness and affliction is reminiscent of the trials of Job.

¹² My friends and comrades keep aloof in my calamity,
and at a distance stand my next of kin.
¹³ And those who seek my life lay snares for me;
and those who wish me evil threaten ruin to me;
they plot intrigues unceasingly.

III ¹⁴ But I — like to one deaf, I do not hear;
like to one dumb that opens not his mouth.
¹⁵ I am become a man that does not hear,
as one that has no answer on his lips.
¹⁶ In you, indeed, O Lord, I trust;
you, Lord, my God, will answer me.
¹⁷ This is my prayer: "Let them not triumph over me;
let them not proudly boast because my foot is faltering."

IV ¹⁸ For I am on the verge of faltering;
day in, day out, my grief confronts me.
¹⁹ Yes, I confess my guilt;
my sin fills me with great anxiety.
²⁰ Those who oppose me unprovoked are men in power;
and numberless are those that hate me wantonly.
²¹ Requiting ill for good, they pester me,
because I strive to do the right.
²² Do not, O Lord, abandon me;
O do not stand aloof from me, my God.
²³ Make haste to bring me help,
my Lord, my savior!

PSALM 38

Laments and Prayers of a Seriously Sick Man

I. Seriously ill, the psalmist wishes to keep his suffering to himself,
lest he might give to wicked men an opportunity of blaspheming,
but he finds that he cannot suppress the anguish of his mind (2–4).
II. He asks God to reveal to him the measure of his days and
meditates on the transitoriness of all men's lives (5–7). III. He hopes
that God will give him pardon for his sins (8, 9). IV. Therefore,
he prays earnestly that God will be merciful to him and preserve
his life (10–14).

¹ *To the choirmaster, Iduthun. A psalm of David.*

I   ² I said: "I shall be watchful of my ways,
      lest I should trespass with my tongue.
      A bridle will I put upon my mouth
      when face to face with a godless man."
    ³ So, wrapt in silence, I let comfort go,
      alas, my grief burst out afresh.
    ⁴ My heart within me warmed;
      as I took thought, the fire blazed forth.
      I spoke out with my tongue.

II   ⁵ Make known to me my end, O Lord —
      what is the measure of my days:
      I wish to know how frail I am.
    ⁶ Alas, my days are but a span — you made them so!
      My life is next to nothing in your reckoning;
      a breath — no more — is every man!
    ⁷ A passing shadow — such is man!
      And all his fretting is about inanities!
      He hoards, not knowing who shall be his heir.

III   ⁸ And now, Lord, what do I expect?
      My trust is all in you!
    ⁹ From all my wrongs deliver me!
      O do not let me be the laughingstock of fools!

IV   ¹⁰ I hold my peace! I open not my mouth!
      It is your doing, after all!
    ¹¹ Remove from me your scourge;
      beneath the impact of your blows I faint away.
    ¹² You chasten man by punishing his sins;
      you ruin, like a moth, all he holds dear.
      A breath, no more, is every man.
    ¹³ Lord, hear my prayer,
      and listen to my cry;
      and to my tearful plea do not be deaf.

38:2. *I shall be watchful of my ways:* i.e., I shall faithfully observe the precepts of God.

38:13 ff. He is speaking here of a brief respite which God may concede to him, after his illness.

A stranger am I in your sight;
a pilgrim as my fathers were.

14 Then turn your frown away from me, and let me breathe,
ere I depart and am no more.

PSALM 39

Thanksgiving and a Prayer for Aid in a New Affliction

A. I. The psalmist asserts that he has always had help from God
(2–4). II. He recalls how many and how great are the blessings
which God has bestowed on him (5, 6). III. The best way of giving
thanks to God, says the psalmist, is to be obedient to his precepts
(7, 9) and to have the desire of making these blessings known to
others (10–11). B. The psalmist's thought now turns to a plea for
aid in a new affliction (12–18). I. He describes the troubles that
now harass him (12, 13). II. He prays that the wicked may be
confounded and good men made happy (14–18).

The last part of this psalm, vv. 14–18, forms the whole of Ps. 69.

1 *To the choirmaster. A psalm of David.*

A I 2 Unswervingly I trusted in the Lord;
and he stooped down to me and heard my cry.

3 He drew me out from deadly pit, from miry hole,
and on a rock he firmly set my feet;
he made my steps secure.

4 He put into my mouth a song not sung before,
a song to praise our God.
And many a one will understand and fear,
and hope in the Lord.

II 5 Well for the man who puts his trust in the Lord,
and does not follow idol-worshipers or men that lean to frauds.

6 Full many are your wondrous deeds, O Lord, my God;
in planning for our weal you have no peer.

38:14b. *ere I . . . am no more:* i.e., in this life. He is not speaking of
the future life here.

39:6b. *in planning . . . you have no peer:* i.e., in kindly providence
and care.

If I should wish to list them all,
they would be past all numbering.

III   7   Oblation or a sacrifice you did not want;
but you have given me an open ear.
Sin offering and holocaust you did not ask;
8   then I declared: "Look; here I am!
Upon the scroll of writing it is said of me:
9   'To do your will, my God, is my delight.'
Your law is written in my heart."
10   In full assembly I announced your just demands;
you know, Lord, very well: I did not check my tongue.
11   Your just demands I did not in my heart conceal;
I blazed abroad your help and your fidelity.
I did not hide your kindliness
or your fidelity when all the people met.

I   12   For your part, Lord, do not withhold your kindliness from me;
your grace and your fidelity — may they preserve me evermore.
13   For, ills past numbering have ringed me round;
my sins have overtaken me — I cannot count them all.
More numerous are they than are the hairs upon my head.
My heart within me sinks.

II   14   Be pleased, O Lord, to rescue me;
make haste to help me, Lord.
15   Discomfiture and shame to all
that seek to take my life!
May all who gloat on my calamity
retreat in utter shame!
16   And may confusion strike those dumb
that say to me: "Ha! Ha!"
17   May all that look to you for help
say in ecstatic joy: "The Lord be glorified!"
18   I am forlorn and poor;
the Lord, however, is concerned for me.
My helper, my deliverer are you;
my God, do not delay.

39:8b. *Upon the scroll of writing:* i.e., in the books of the Old Testament.

Psalm 40

Confidence and Prayer of a Sick Man

I. The psalmist, stricken with illness, remembers that it is the merciful who receive mercy; this thought strengthens him (2–4). II. No hope is to be placed in man. His enemies eagerly await and pray for his death, and even an intimate friend treats him treacherously (5–10). III. Hence, he seeks from God alone restoration of health and victory over his foes (11–13). Verse 14 is the doxology which closes Book 1 of the Psalms.

1 *To the choirmaster. A psalm of David.*

I   2 Blest is he who keeps in mind the wretched poor:
the Lord will save him on his evil day.
3 The Lord will shield him, save his life,
and make him happy on the earth;
he will not let his enemies do what they want with him.
4 The Lord will bring him help upon his bed of pain,
and in his illness take away all his infirmity.

II   5 I say: O Lord, have mercy on me;
I sinned against you: heal me, then.
6 My enemies speak ill of me:
"When will he die? When will his name be blotted out?"
7 When someone comes to visit me, he speaks but hollow words;
meanwhile he gathers venom in his heart, and, gone outdoors,
speaks out.
8 To injure me, my enemies join in whisperings;
to injure me, they harbor evil thoughts:
9 "A virulent plague has been let loose on him!"
Again, "Once on his back, he will arise no more!"
10 My friend, my confidant, who ate my bread —
he, too, now lifts his heel to injure me.

III   11 But you, Lord, pity me and raise me up;
that I may pay them back!

40:3. This verse, put in the form of a petition, is used by the Church as a prayer for the Supreme Pontiff.

12 Then shall I know that you are pleased with me
   when my opponent does not triumph over me.
13 You will preserve me hale and strong,
   and keep your loving eye on me forevermore.

14 Blest be the Lord, the God of Israel,
   from age to age! So be it! Be it so!

BOOK 2: Psalms 41-71

Psalms 41 and 42

The Desire to Be With God in His Holy Temple

This and the following psalm are to be taken as one psalm; the thought and form (note the repetition in 41:6 and 42:5) and the lack of a separate inscription for Psalm 42 indicate this.

I. The psalmist, a levite, driven into exile by the underhandedness of wicked men (cf. 42:1), and desiring to return to the temple, sorrowfully recalls how he had participated in its jubilant solemnities, and he trusts that once again he may honor God in festal joy (2–6). II. Borne down by grief, and laughed at by his enemies because of his trust in God, he sheds tears night and day (7–12). III. Sincerely he asks God to defend him and lead him back to the temple, that there he may once more utter his praises (42:1–5).

Psalm 41

¹ *To the choirmaster. A maskil of the sons of Core.*

I ² As deer will yearn for running brook,
so yearns my soul for you, O God.
³ I am athirst for God, the living God:
when may I come and see God's face?
⁴ My tears are bread to me both day and night;
for daily I am asked: "Where is your God?"
⁵ This I recall, as I to sadness yield my soul:
how once I marched in pilgrimage on the way to the house of God!
What cries of praise and jubilee encircled us!
How festive was the gathering!
⁶ *O why are you depressed, my soul?*
And why this tumult in my breast?
Have trust in God: once again shall I honor him with festal joy,
my God, my savior, and my comforter!

41:1. *maskil:* the term is found in the title of some thirteen psalms. Its meaning is not clear. The most acceptable explanation is that it means a skillful, ingenious psalm.

II 7 My inmost spirits are depressed.
I therefore think of you in the land of Jordan and Hermon, on
    Misar Hill!
  8 Deep calls on deep amid your roaring cataracts,
and all your rolling waves are passing over me.
  9 O may the Lord in daytime grant his grace,
and I will sing to him at night, and praise the God who is my life.
 10 I say to God: My rock, why, why are you forgetting me?
Why must I go about disconsolate, afflicted by my foe?
 11 My frame is shaken when my foes make sport of me,
and when they daily taunt: "Where is your God?"
 12 *O why are you depressed, my soul?*
And why this tumult in my breast?
Have trust in God: once again shall I honor him with festal joy,
my God, my savior, and my comforter!

PSALM 42

III 1 O do me justice, God,
take up my cause against unholy people.
From wicked and deceitful men deliver me.
  2 You are my strength, O God:
O why have you rejected me?
Why must I go about disconsolate, afflicted by my foe?
  3 Send forth your kindly light and plighted help: may they my
    escort be,
and lead me to your dwelling place upon your holy mount.
  4 Go in I will and face the altar of God,
face God, my joy and ecstasy.
And I will praise you with the cither,
O God, my God!
  5 *O why are you depressed, my soul?*
And why this tumult in my breast?

41:7. The psalmist describes the place in which he is composing the psalm; it is near the spot where the Jordan takes its source at the foot of Mount Hermon. Misar Hill was probably some smaller mountain nearby.

41:8. The roar of the cataracts of the Jordan in the narrow valley, where it takes its rise, suggests to the psalmist the flood of troubles with which he is overwhelmed.

*Have trust in God: once again shall I honor him with festal joy,
my God, my savior, and my comforter!*

The People of Israel, Once Protected by God,
but Now Repudiated by Him, Seek His Help

I. The people of Israel remember that happy time when God was their leader and preserved them safe when they were under attack (2–9). II. They compare with those good days the present doleful time, when, repulsed by God and conquered by enemies, they are sold into servitude and made the laughingstock of all (10–17). III. They hold that this happened because they were always faithful to God (18–23). IV. Therefore they ask God to turn to them again in mercy (24–27).

¹ To the choirmaster. A maskil of the sons of Core.

I ² O God, with our own ears we heard;
our fathers told us of the work
which you accomplished in their days,
in days of old!
³ The heathen driven out, your hand then settled them;
the nations crushed, you gave them ample room.
⁴ Not by their sword did they possess the land;
'twas not their arm delivered them;
but your right hand and your own arm it was;
your kindly smile: you took them to your heart.
⁵ You are my king, my God;
the victories of Jacob were your gift.
⁶ Through you we have repulsed our foes,
and in your name we trampled on our enemies.
⁷ No, no, I did not trust in my own bow;
'twas not my sword delivered me.
⁸ But you — you saved us from our foes;
and those who hated us you put to shame.
⁹ In God we gloried all the time;
we never ceased to praise your name.

II ¹⁰ But now you shamed us and discarded us!
And with our hosts you sally forth no more, O God.

¹¹ You made us yield to our antagonists;
our foes enriched themselves by plundering us!

¹² Like sheep for slaughter did you give us over;
among the heathens you have scattered us.

¹³ Without a price you sold your chosen race:
and little gain there was for you in selling them.

¹⁴ You made of us a byword for our neighbors;
mocked are we and scorned by those that live around us.

¹⁵ Topic for talk you made of us among the heathenish folk;
in scorn the nations shake their heads at us.

¹⁶ My shame forever stares me in the face,
and blushes mantle on my cheeks,

¹⁷ because we are reviled and mocked,
and men make open war with us.

III ¹⁸ All this came down on us though we had not forgotten you;
nor did we violate your covenant.

¹⁹ Our heart had not relinquished you,
nor had our steps deflected from your path,

²⁰ the time you crushed us in the place of our affliction,
and with a pall of darkness covered us.

²¹ Had we forgotten our own God's name
and stretched out hands to an alien god,

²² would not our God have searched this out?
He knows the secrets of the heart.

²³ But for your sake we always are being done to death;
as sheep for slaughter are we now accounted.

IV ²⁴ Rise, Lord! Why do you sleep?
Awake! Do not discard us utterly!

²⁵ Why do you hide your face?
And why forget our misery and grief?

²⁶ We have been humbled to the dust;
we grovel in the dirt.

²⁷ Then rise to bring us help;
and save us for your mercy's sake!

PSALM 44

A Nuptial Song for the King, the Messias

I. In the prologue, the solemn song is dedicated to the king (2).
II. The psalmist addresses the king (3–10): he proclaims his beauty
(3, 4), his strength (5, 6), his justice (7, 8), his riches and magnificence (9, 10). III. Then he turns to the queen (11–16): he advises
her to devote herself totally to the king, for which honor will come
to her (11–13). He describes the queen. She is elegantly garbed
and surrounded by her maidens, as she makes her royal entry
(14–16). IV. In the epilogue, he predicts for the king a long progeny
and perpetual glory (17, 18).

From Hebr. 1:8, 9, and from the whole of Christian as well
as Jewish tradition, it is evident that the king is the Messias; the
queen, therefore, is his spouse, the Church (cf. Eph. 5:25–27). In
describing the king and queen, the psalmist may have had in mind
the nuptials of some king with a princess from a neighboring country
which had been celebrated with pomp in his day.

1   *To the choirmaster. To the melody, "The Lilies." A maskil of
the sons of Core. A love song.*

I   2   My heart pours forth a noble song;
I chant my paean to the king.
My tongue is like a rapid writer's quill.

II   3   Beyond all mortals you are fair of form;
your lips are bathed in loveliness.
God's blessing will be yours in all eternity.
4   Now gird your sword upon your thigh, most mighty king;
and don your armor bright and beautiful.
5   Ride forth to champion justice and fidelity;
your right arm teach you great exploits.
6   Sharp are your shafts; the nations bow to you;
the enemies of the king are losing heart.
7   Your throne, O God, stands for eternity;
your regal sceptre is a sceptre of equity.
8   You love the right and hate the wrong;
therefore has God, your God, anointed you with oil
of gladness more than all your fellow kings.

9 Fragrant are your robes with aloe, cassia, myrrh;
   from ivory palaces a strain of strings caresses you.
10 To meet your glance, daughters of kings approach;
   the queen stands at your right, arrayed in Ophir gold.

III 11 List, daughter: look, and lend your ear;
   forget your nation and your father's house.
12 Your beauty will enchant the king:
   he is your Lord; your homage pay to him.
13 The Tyrian folk advance with gifts;
   the noblest of the people woo your smile.
14 All fair, the daughter of a king is entering;
   her vesture is of cloth of gold.
15 In rich embroidery robed, she is presented to the king;
   the maidens in her train, her friends, are introduced to you.
16 They are led in with rapturous joy,
   and wend their way into the palace of the king.

IV 17 You shall have sons to take your parents' place,
   and shall appoint them rulers of the world.
18 I will make known your name in every age to come,
   and thus the nations shall acclaim you everlastingly.

PSALM 45

God, Our Defense and Strength

I. God is with us; nothing terrifies us (2–4). II. God is in the midst of the Holy City; no attack can devastate it (5–8). III. God, the Most High, puts an end to wars (9–12).
   The psalm was probably composed for celebrating the liberation of Jerusalem from the blockade of Sennacherib (cf. Kings 4:18–19).

1 *To the choirmaster. Of the sons of Core. To the melody, "The Virgins." A song.*

44:10. There is a transition here to a description of the entrance of the queen with her retinue.
   44:10b. *Ophir:* a region situated on the seacoast of Arabia or east Africa, from which the ships of Solomon brought gold.
   44:13. *Tyrian folk:* the Tyrians here stand for foreigners.
   44:17. The psalmist addresses the king, not the queen, in the last verses.

I   ² God is our refuge and our strength;
a mighty helper in distress he proved himself.

    ³ Therefore we do not fear: should e'en the earth turn upside down
and mountains crash into mid-sea!

    ⁴ Yes, let its waters surge and seethe,
let mountains shake beneath its shock:
the Lord of hosts is on our side;
the God of Jacob is our shield!

II   ⁵ A flowing river cheers the citadel of God
— the holiest tent of the Most High!

    ⁶ For in its midst is God: it stands unmoved;
God to its rescue runs at early dawn.

    ⁷ The Gentiles raved, and kingdoms shook;
then roared his thunder voice: the earth dissolved!

    ⁸ *The Lord of hosts is on our side;*
the God of Jacob is our shield.

III ⁹ Then come; see what the Lord has done,
the wonders he has wrought on earth:

  ¹⁰ he curbs all wars throughout the world;
he shatters bows; he shivers spears; he burns to ashes shields.

  ¹¹ Desist! Acknowledge me as God,
supreme among the nations, supreme on earth.

  ¹² *The Lord of hosts is on our side;*
the God of Jacob is our shield.

PSALM 46

God, the Victorious King, Ascends His Throne

I. God, mighty king, subjects all nations to his people (2–5). II. After the victory, he ascends his throne (6, 7). III. Now he rules over

---

45:5. See Gen. 2:10–14, concerning the river of paradise, a *flowing river*, as it is here termed. Note the contrast between the surging, threatening sea and the peaceful, flowing river which cheers the city of God.

(One critic says that he does not see the value of referring to Gen. 2:10–14. He explains: "If the psalm was written after Sennacherib's invasion, the reference is more likely to be to the contemporary prophet Isaias, who in 8:6, 33:21, and 66:12 compares God's government of his people to a river of peace, a silently flowing stream. God Himself is like a mighty river, which surrounds and protects the Holy City." — *T. J. L.*)

all nations, all princes and powerful ones of the earth (8–10).

The psalm refers to the ultimate victory of God and the institution of the universal messianic kingdom. Israel and the Gentiles will constitute one kingdom of the Messias.

1 *To the choirmaster. Of the sons of Core. A psalm.*

I 2 All peoples, clap your hands;
exult in God with festive cries.
3 High-throning, dreadful is the Lord,
a mighty king o'er all the earth.
4 The peoples he subdues to us,
and lays the nations at our feet.
5 For us he chooses as our heritage
the pride of Jacob, whom he loves.

II 6 God mounts with jubilant cries,
the Lord, with trumpet blare.
7 Sing psalms to God; sing psalms;
sing psalms to our King; sing psalms.

III 8 Indeed, the king of all the earth is God.
Intone a hymn!
9 God sways the nations;
God sits upon his holy throne.
10 The rulers of the nations are united with
the people of Abraham's God.
Indeed, God's vassals are the princes of the earth;
he is transcendently supreme.

PSALM 47

God's Glory Manifested in the Deliverance of the Holy City

I. After Jerusalem, by an evident intervention of God, has been freed from the attack of certain kings who had leagued themselves against it (cf. vv. 5–7), the psalmist sings the praise of God, who had so powerfully protected his Holy City (2–4). II. He describes the shock, terror, and flight of the enemy kings (5–8). III. He

---

46:10. The Gentiles and the people of Abraham are now one people.

introduces pilgrims coming from afar to the temple and praising God because of the deliverance that had been obtained (9–12). IV. He invites these pilgrims to inspect the city that was preserved undamaged and to tell future generations about this miracle performed by God (13–15).

¹ A song. A psalm. Of the sons of Core.

I   ² Great is the Lord and highly to be praised —
within the city of our God!
   ³ His holy mount — a noble hill —
it is the joy of all the earth.
Mount Sion — the outmost north —
it is the great King's citadel.
   ⁴ God in its fastnesses
has proved himself a sure defense.

II   ⁵ Mark well: the kings, together leagued,
had made a joint attack.
   ⁶ They saw — at once they were amazed,
and helter-skelter fled away!
   ⁷ Yes, trembling seized them there and then,
a pain as of a woman in her pangs;
   ⁸ it was as when the east wind
shatters the Tharsian fleet.

III   ⁹ As we heard, so we have seen,
within the city of the Lord of hosts,
within the city of our God:
God makes her strong forevermore!
   ¹⁰ Your mercy, God, we gratefully recall
within your holy shrine.
   ¹¹ As does your name, O God, so does your praise
reach to the earth's extremity.
With justice overflows your hand:

47:3c. Assyrian mythology held that the "mount of the gods" was in the far north. Hence, the psalmist means that Sion is the true mount of the north, where the true God dwells.

47:8b. Tharsian ships were the large merchant vessels that plied the Mediterranean between Palestine and Tartessus in the southwest of Spain. Though they were rugged vessels, they could not stand up against the strong east wind, which was noted for its destructiveness.

¹² O may the Sion Hill rejoice,
and Juda's cities leap for joy,
since your awards are just!

IV ¹³ Walk through Sion, all around it walk,
and count its battlements;
¹⁴ inspect its engines of defense;
review its bulwarks, one by one,
that to the future generation you may say:
¹⁵ "So great is God,
our God forever and forevermore!
'Tis he will shepherd us!"

PSALM 48

Men Wonder at the Prosperity of Sinners

This psalm treats, as does Psalm 36, of the question of the prosperity
that wicked men so often enjoy.

In the introduction, the psalmist calls on all men to hearken to
him (2–5). I. He notes that all men, even the wealthiest, must
die and leave their riches behind them (6–12). II. He says further
that the lot of wicked men is with the dead in eternal ruin; good
men, however, are taken to the heart of God and will reign with
him forever (14–20). The main thought is repeated in vv. 13, 21.

¹ *To the choirmaster. Of the sons of Core. A psalm.*

² Hear this, O nations one and all;
give ear, all you who dwell upon the globe,
³ alike the humbly and the nobly born,
the rich as well as poor.
⁴ My mouth will utter wisdom;
the meditation of my heart, intelligence!
⁵ To hear things hidden will I lend my ear,
and bare my secret to the harp's accompaniment.

I ⁶ Why should I fear in troublous times,
when plotters' craft encircles me?
⁷ Their trust is in their wealth;
their vast resources are their boast.
⁸ Truly, no man can liberate himself,
or pay a ransom price to God!

9 The ransom of his life is more than he can pay;
   nor will it ever be enough,
10 that he may live on in eternity
   and never see the grave.
11 He surely sees that wise men die,
   that fools and blockheads perish equally,
   and leave their wealth to other hands.
12 The sepulchres are their eternal homes,
   their dwelling place from age to age,
   though with their names they labelled their estates!
13 *In spite of wealth, no man can last;*
   he is like to cattle — doomed to pass away!

II 14 Such is the fate of self-reliant fools;
      such, too, the end of men enamored of their lot.
   15 Like sheep, penned up they are in hell;
      death is their shepherd; their masters are the just.
      Soon will their glory be effaced,
      and hell will be their home.
   16 But God will save my soul from hell;
      for he will take me to his heart.
   17 O do not fear if someone gains in riches,
      or if his house grows opulent;
   18 for when he dies, he will take nought with him,
      nor will his wealth go down with him.
   19 In life he styled himself a happy man:
      "They will speak well of you! You certainly enjoyed yourself!"
   20 Yet will he join his fathers' company,
      who are to see the light of day no more!
   21 *A man who lives in opulence and is not wise*
      is like to cattle, doomed to pass away.

PSALM 49

Concerning the Right Worship of God

The psalmist is opposed to a merely external worship, one which
is lacking in true interior obedience to the law of God.
   I. He presents God as appearing for a solemn judgment (1–6).

II. God now speaks to the people, saying that he does not need sacrifices, but he does demand thanksgiving and petitions for divine aid (7–15). III. Then, turning to a sinner, he condemns him for giving lip service to the law of God, while in his way of living, he openly violates it (16–21). IV. God demands gratitude and obedience; if these are lacking, a man will be lost (22, 23).

¹ *A psalm of Asaph.*

I   The Lord God's voice has summoned the earth
       from sunrise to its setting.
² On radiant Sion Mount has God appeared.
³ Our God has come! He does not hold his peace!
       Devouring fire marks his advance;
       round him a tempest roars.
⁴ He summons heaven above and all the earth;
       he is to judge his chosen race:
⁵ "Summon together my saints for me —
       who ratified my pact with sacrifice!"
⁶ The heavens proclaim his justice;
       for God — none other — is the judge!

II ⁷ "My people, list; and I will speak;
       list, Israel; against you will I testify!
       For God, your God, I am!
⁸ 'Tis not your sacrifices that I reprimand;
       your holocausts are offered me unceasingly.
⁹ Yet will I have no bullock from your stock,
       no he-goat from your herd.
¹⁰ Mine are the beasts that rove the woods,
       the thousands of beasts upon my hills.
¹¹ I well know all the birds upon the wing;
       whatever roams the fields is known to me.
¹² If I am hungry, shall I tell you so?
       Mine is the globe and all that fills it.
¹³ Need I to eat the flesh of bulls,
       or drink the blood of goats?
¹⁴ No, offer up to God a sacrifice of praise,
       and pay to the Most High your vows;
¹⁵ then call on me in time of sore distress;
       and deliver you I will, because you honor me."

III 16 But to the sinner God speaks thus:
         "Why do you tell the tale of my commands,
         and glibly talk about my covenant —
     17 yes, you who hate my warning voice
         and cast my teaching to the winds?
     18 You saw a thief: you ran along with him;
         you freely mingled with adulterers.
     19 You gave your tongue free rein for evil speech;
         your mouth framed treacherous plans.
     20 In company, you ridiculed your brother;
         you slandered your own mother's son.
     21 All this you did; and I shall hold my peace?
         Did you suppose that I resembled you?
         You I blame, and cast your conduct in your teeth.

IV   22 Think of this, all you who do not think of God;
         else I will snatch you off, with none to bring you help.
     23 He honors me who offers me a sacrifice of praise;
         whoever lives aright, him will I save as only God can save."

PSALM 50

Confession of a Penitent Sinner;
His Promises and Petitions

In the introduction (A) the psalmist asks for remission of his
sins (3, 4). (B) I. In the body of the psalm, he confesses that he
has sinned, indeed, that he was born in sin, that sincerity demands
this confession (5–8). II. He asks that he may be received back into
grace (9–11). III. He begs that God will give him a spirit of
perseverance (12–14). IV. He mentions reasons which should impel
God to forgive him: the zeal he has for converting others, his
offering to God of a contrite heart (15–19). In C, there is added a
brief prayer that Jerusalem may be rebuilt and worship restored
there (20, 21). This is the fourth of the penitential psalms.

 1 *To the choirmaster. A psalm of David,* 2 *when the prophet
    Nathan came to reproach him for his sin with Bethsabee.*

 3 Have mercy on me, God, for you are merciful;
    blot out my sin, for you are richly merciful.

⁴ Completely cleanse me from my guilt,
and purge me from my sin.

B I ⁵ Yes, I acknowledge my iniquity;
my sin at all times stares me in the face.
⁶ 'Twas you alone 'gainst whom I sinned;
what in your sight is evil — that I did!
You must be shown to have been in your sentence just,
and in your judgment, right.
⁷ Alas, I was in sin when I was born,
in sin, too, when I was conceived.
⁸ But now — sincerity of heart is your delight;
deep-searching wisdom you impart to me.

II ⁹ With hyssop sprinkle me: I shall be clean;
wash me: and I shall whiter be than snow.
¹⁰ O let me hear the good and joyful word;
you crushed my frame: O let it now be thrilled!
¹¹ O turn your face away from my misdeeds,
and blot out all my guilt.

III ¹² A heart all pure create in me, O God;
a spirit new and firm breathe into me.
¹³ No, do not from your presence banish me;
your Holy Spirit do not take away from me.
¹⁴ Restore to me the joy which your salvation brings;
and by a generous spirit make me strong.

IV ¹⁵ I will instruct the wicked in your ways;
and sinners will turn back to you.
¹⁶ Free me from the penalty for bloodshed, God, my savior God;
and let my tongue exult by reason of your clemency.

50:6. The essential nature of sin is that it is an offense against God; every other aspect of it is secondary.

50:7. Man's tendency to sin comes from his origin. Catholic tradition holds that the doctrine of original sin is indicated here.

50:9. Hyssop was an herb that was cultivated along garden walls in oriental gardens. Its branches, gathered into a small brush and dipped into the blood of a sacrificial victim, were used for aspersion, in such liturgical rites as the purifying of the unclean.

50:16. The psalmist seems to recall the slaying of Urias (2 Sam. 11:6–17; 12:9).

17 Open my lips, O Lord;
   my tongue will hymn your praise.
18 'Tis not with sacrifice that you are pleased,
   and if I offered holocausts, you would not care for them.
19 A contrite spirit is my sacrifice, O God;
   a crushed and humbled heart, O God, you will not loathe.

C 20 Deal kindly, Lord, with Sion in your graciousness;
   rebuild the ramparts of Jerusalem.
21 And then you will receive the lawful sacrifices, offerings and
   holocausts;
   then bullocks will be on your altar laid.

PSALM 51

Against a Rich and Influential Calumniator

I. The malice of the calumniator (3–6). II. The punishment of
eternal ruin is predicted for him (7). III. The just will rejoice and
give thanks (8–11).

1 To the choirmaster. A maskil of David,
2 after Doeg, the Edomite, had come to Saul and told him: "David
   has gone into Abimelech's house."

I 3 Why do you glory in maliciousness,
   O ill-famed overlord?
4 You brood on mischief all the time;
   your tongue, O master of deceit,
   is like a sharpened knife!
5 You cherish evil more than good,
   and lying more than honest utterance!
6 Deceitful tongue,
   your sole delight is wicked speech!

II 7 And therefore God will ruin you,
   and make away with you for all eternity.
   Yes, he will snatch you from your tent,
   and drive you from the land of the living.

50:18. Sacrifices in atonement for homicide and adultery were not prescribed, nor were they in use; such sins were punished by death, but David,
since he was king, could not be put to death.

III 8 The good will see it, and will fear;
and they will taunt the man:
   9 "Here is a man that did not, once for all,
make God his guardian,
but put his trust in his abundant wealth
and gathered strength from wickedness."
  10 But I am like a blooming olive tree within the house of God;
my trust is in God's mercy everlastingly.
  11 Forever will I sing your praise, because you intervened;
and I will celebrate your name — for it is good —
when all the saints foregather.

Psalm 52

The Depravity of All Men and Their Punishment

This psalm is almost identical with Psalm 13. The faithless Israelites
fear the Assyrians more than they fear God, whom they should
have feared.

   1 *To the choirmaster. To the melody of "Mahalat." A maskil
of David.*

I 2 The fool says in his heart:
"There is no God!"
The world is vile, and shocking are its ways!
There is not one who acts aright!
   3 From heaven God looks out upon the human race
to see if there is one wise man that seeks for God!
   4 No, all the world has strayed and is depraved;
there is not one who acts aright — not one!

II 5 Will not the wicked world return to sanity?
They eat my people up, as they eat bread!
They do not worship God!
   6 They trembled once in fear

51:11. *because you intervened:* i.e., by punishing the calumniator.

there, where there was no cause for fear,
because God strewed about the bones of your beleaguerers;
these scurried off in shame since God discarded them!

III   7   Would that from Sion came the weal of Israel!
When God has changed the fortunes of his race,
then Jacob will hold jubilee, then Israel will rejoice!

PSALM 53

A Prayer for God's Help Against Enemies

I. Enemies seek to kill the psalmist. He asks for help against these men (3–5). II. Certain that his prayer has been heard, he, at once, promises sacrifices and thanksgiving to God (6–9).

1 *To the choirmaster. For stringed instruments. A maskil of David,*
2 *when the men of Ziph came to Saul and told him: "David is hidden among us."*

I   3   God, in your name deliver me,
and by your might defend my cause.
4 God, hear my prayer;
hear with attention what I say.
5 For, proud men are assailing me,
and violent men have sought my life.
They never think of God.

II   6   And yet, God is my help;
the Lord sustains my life.
7 See that their evil deeds recoil upon my foes;
and may your plighted word destroy them all!
8 Then will I gladly sacrifice to you,
and hymn your name, O Lord; for it is good.
9 Indeed, from all distress he rescued me,
and my own eye beheld my foes discomfited.

53:3. *name:* here stands for the power of God.

PSALM 54

Against His Enemies and a Certain Faithless Friend

I. The psalmist is in fear and anguish because of the attacks of his enemies; he is anxious to find a haven from the storm (2–9). II. He bewails the discord and oppression which disturb the city; he is distressed particularly by the faithlessness of a certain friend (10–15). III. He ardently hopes for the ruin of his enemies and his own liberation; he stirs himself to greater trust in God (16–24).

1 *To the choirmaster. For stringed instruments. A maskil of David.*

I 2 To my prayer, O God, give ear;
and from my pleading do not turn away.

3 O heed and answer me;
I am perplexed in my distress;

4 I am bewildered by my enemy's talk,
and by the sinner's noisy threats.
They do me wrong
and in their anger harass me.

5 My inmost heart is terrified;
the dread of death is overshadowing me.

6 Trembling and fear come over me;
a pall of horror covers me.

7 I say: "Would I had wings as has a dove;
then should I fly away and be at rest.

8 Indeed, I should go far away,
and settle in the wilderness.

9 Refuge I should seek at once
from whirlwind and from storm."

II 10 Lord, scatter them! Divide their tongues!
For in the city I see violence and strife.

11 And day and night they go about it on its walls;
wrong and oppression flourish in its midst.

12 And in its midst are pitfalls laid;

54:10. *Divide their tongues:* i.e., throw them into confusion, into discord (cf. Gen. 11:6–9).

54:10–12. These verses may refer to the sedition of Absalom and the disorders that sprang from it (2 Sam. 15); what follows refers to Achitophel (2 Sam. 16:15–23).

and in its streets are rampant wrong and fraud.

13 Had but an enemy insulted me,
I should have borne up patiently;
had one who hates me rushed on me,
I should have hid myself from him.

14 But it was you, my comrade,
friend, and confidant!

15 Our comradeship — what feast it was for me!
In God's own house we walked amid the festive throng!

III 16 May death rush on them all!
Alive may they go down to hell!
Their homes, their lives are steeped in wickedness.

17 But I will cry to God;
the Lord will rescue me!

18 At even, morn, and noon, I will lament and groan;
and he will hear my voice,

19 and save me from my foes, restore my peace of soul;
for many they are that combat me.

20 God will hear, and put them down — for he is King from all
eternity.
They do not mend their ways; they do not reverence God!

21 Not one of them but reaches out his hands to hurt his friends;
not one but violates his pact.

22 More smooth than butter is their face;
yet in their heart lurks strife.
More soft than oil are all their words,
yet like they are to drawn swords.

23 O cast upon the Lord your care,
and he will bear you up.
He never will permit a saint to fall.

24 And you, O God, will bring them down
into the deadly pit.

54:15b. *amid the festive throng:* this seems to refer to the solemn processions to the temple. The meaning, therefore, is: we were most closely associated in both private and religious life.
54:21. Cf. vv. 13–15; the disloyalty of a friend grieves him more than the deceits of enemies.

Bloodthirsty and deceitful men will never live out half their days.
But I put trust in you, O Lord.

PSALM 55

When Oppressed, the Psalmist Places
Full Trust in God

Surrounded on all sides by enemies, the psalmist continues to place
his confidence in God. This is brought out in the refrains in vv. 5
and 11.
    I. When assailed by enemies, the psalmist does not fear (2–4).
II. Attacked by them, he asks God to be mindful of him in this
crisis and to help him (6–10). III. Once freed from this distress,
he will fulfill a vow of thanksgiving (13, 14).

1 *To the choirmaster. To the melody, "Yonat Elem Rehoquim."*
   A miktam. When the Philistines held him captive in Gath.

I   2 Have mercy on me, O God; men trample me!
     Forever they oppress and combat me!
   3 My foes forever trample me;
     so many they are that combat me!
   4 Most High, the day when fear steals over me
     in you I put my trust.
   5 *In God, whose promises I hymn with thanks,*
     in God I trust: I shall not fear;
     for what can mortal do to me!

II   6 The livelong day they speak but ill of me;
     and all their thoughts are bent on hurting me!
   7 They meet in cliques; they lie in wait;
     my steps they watch; they seek my life.
   8 Repay them for their evil deeds;
     God, in your anger, lay the nations low.
   9 You mark my life of banishment;
     my tears are treasured in your reservoir;
     and are they not recorded in your book?
  10 Then will my enemies retreat
     when I have called on you.

   54:24c. *Bloodthirsty . . . men will never live out half their days:* they
will not reach a full span of life; they will die prematurely (cf. Ps. 101:25).
   55:9b. *in your reservoir:* God carefully collects every tear.

This well I know, that God is on my side.
¹¹ *In God, whose promises I hymn with thanks,*
¹² *in God I trust; I shall not fear;*
for what can mortal do to me!

III ¹³ Bound by the vows I made to you, O God,
I will perform the sacrifice of praise,
¹⁴ because you snatched my life from death,
my feet from slipping;
and thus, beneath God's eye, I live in the sunshine of this life.

PSALM 56

In the Midst of Persecution, the Psalmist Is All Trustful

The refrain in vv. 6 and 12 divides the psalm into two parts. I. In the first part, the psalmist, buoyed up by hope, asks God's help against enemies who press him on all sides (2–5). II. In the second part, certain of being saved, he at once thanks God (7–12).

With a few changes, vv. 8–12 constitute the first part of Psalm 107.

¹ *To the choirmaster. To the melody, "Do not Destroy." A maskil of David. When he fled into a cave from Saul.*

I ² Be merciful to me, O God; be merciful!
To you I have recourse with all my heart.
The shadow of your wings is my retreat
until disaster passes by.
³ I raise my voice to God Most High,
to God, who is beneficent to me.
⁴ May he from heaven send deliverance to me,
and shame my persecutors, each and all.
O may God send his grace and faithfulness!
⁵ I lie down in the midst of lions,
who greedily devour men's flesh;
their teeth are spears and arrows;
their tongue is a sharp sword.

55:14. Cf. Ps. 114:9.

⁶ God, show yourself in heaven on high,
and may your glory shine on all the earth.

II ⁷ A snare they laid to trap my steps;
my spirits they depressed;
they dug a pitfall in my path:
may they fall into it!
⁸ My heart is strong, O God; strong is my heart;
with song and lyre I jubilate.
⁹ Awake, my soul! Awaken, song and lyre!
I will arouse the dawn!
¹⁰ Among the nations will I praise you, Lord;
among the nations sing a song to you!
¹¹ As high as heaven is your kindliness,
high as the clouds your faithfulness!
¹² God, show yourself in heaven on high;
and may your glory shine on all the earth!

PSALM 57

A Rebuke for Unjust Judges

I. The psalmist fiercely denounces unjust judges, whose misuse of their authority results in monstrous injustice (2–6). II. Against such men he invokes divine justice so that, from their punishment, men may come to know that there is a just reward for men of honor and principles (7–12).

¹ To the choirmaster. To the melody, "Do not Destroy." A miktam of David.

I ² Do you, high judges, justly execute the law?
Do you, frail men, make just awards?
³ No, no; at heart you meditate iniquity;
your hands dispense injustice in the land!
⁴ From mother's lap, the godless men have erred;
from mother's womb, all liars went astray.

56:9b. The meaning is: I will arise so early that my song will seem to awaken the dawn. The dawn, too, praises God, but the psalmist will anticipate its praise.

5 They have a venom like the serpent's bane,
  like to the deaf asp's bane that stops its ears
6 lest it should hear the charmer's voice,
  the conjurer's, who skillfully invokes a spell.

II 7 God, crush the teeth within their jaws;
       shatter, O Lord, the lions' molar teeth!
    8 Let them dissolve like water that runs off;
       and if they aim their shafts, let these be blunt.
    9 Like snails that melt away — so let them pass away,
       like an abortive child that never sees the light.
   10 Before your kettles feel the tinder brush,
       while it is green, may then a burning whirlwind snatch it off!
   11 The good man will rejoice on seeing vengeance wreaked,
       and he will lave his feet in sinners' gore.
   12 And then the world will say: "Yes, innocence has its reward;
       assuredly, there is a God that judges here on earth!"

PSALM 58

Against Grasping and Bloodthirsty Enemies

The psalm is divided into two parts (I: 2–11a; II: 11b–18), both
of which close with a refrain (7, 10; 15, 18).
  I. In the first part, the psalmist describes the treachery of his
enemies and asks for God's help (2–6); in the refrain, he compares
these enemies to dogs prowling about seeking food. II. In the second
part the psalmist prays even more urgently that God will scatter and
destroy these foes (11b–14).

57:5–6. Their heart is, as it were, poisoned; they are unwilling to hear
counsels or threats.
  57:10. The figure of the kettles and the tinder brush is taken from the
customs of oriental shepherds, who, in preparing meals in the open, heated
their cooking vessels over a fire of brambles and thorns; and so, not seldom,
before the brush began to burn and to be "felt" by the kettles, a violent
wind would sweep it away. The application here is: with like suddenness,
may wicked judges be destroyed.
  57:11b. The metaphor is taken from wartime usage. A soldier, to obtain
victory, would walk through the spilt blood of the dead and wounded (cf.
Ps. 67:24).

1 *To the choirmaster. To the melody, "Do not Destroy." A miktam of David. When Saul sent men to watch David's house so that they could kill him.*

I   2 Save me from my enemies, my God;
from my assailants shelter me.
3 Save me from men determined to do wrong;
from men that thirst for blood deliver me.
4 Alas, they plot against my life,
and, in their might, conspire to do me harm.
I am not guilty, Lord, of either crime or sin;
5 without my fault they rush to the attack.
Awake! Speed to my aid! See what they do,
6 for you, O Lord of hosts, are Israel's God!
Arise, chastise the nations, one and all;
and do not spare one treacherous fiend!
7 *At evening they return; they yelp like dogs,
and prowl about the city's premises.*
8 O listen how they boast and brag and rail:
"Why, no one cares!"
9 But you, Lord, mock at them;
you hold all nations up to ridicule.
10 *My strength! To you I look.
You, God, are my defense,*
11 *my God, my mercy-seat!*

II   May God come to my aid,
that I may triumph o'er my foes.
12 Slay them, O God; else they will prove your people's stumbling block;
break up their ranks by force, and lay them low,
O Lord, our shield!
13 As many words, so many sins are theirs:
and may their pride, their curses, and their lies be their own snares;
14 Destroy, destroy them in your wrath; and wipe them out:
it must be known that God is King in Jacob and in all the world.

58:7 and 15. They seek their victims as did the dogs which had free run in oriental towns and which, especially in the evenings, prowled the streets in search of food.

58:13. All their speech is sinful.

15 At evening they return; they yelp like dogs;
and prowl about the city's premises.
16 They roam about in quest of food;
and when they do not get their fill, they howl.
17 But I will hymn the praises of your might;
your mercy will inspire my morning song,
because you have become my shield
and refuge in my day of need.
18 My strength, I sing a song to you!
You, God, are my defense,
my God, my mercy-seat!

PSALM 59

Lamentation, Confidence, Prayers
After a Disaster Suffered by the People

I. The psalmist describes the cruel destruction which the people
have suffered and he asks for aid in a new battle (3–7). II. He recalls
the promises in which God had said that all the neighboring tribes
would be subject to the Israelites (8–10). III. He begs God to help
his people now (11–14). Verses 8–14 make up the second part of
Psalm 107.

1 To the choirmaster. To the melody, "The Lily of the Law." A
miktam of David.
2 This happened when he went forth against the Syrians of Ma-
haraim and Soba, and when Joab, on the way back, defeated
the Edomites in the Valley of Salt, twelve thousand of them.

I 3 O God, you beat us back! You broke our battle lines!
You were enraged! Restore us now!
4 You shook the earth; you cleaved it open!
Now heal its ruptures; for it reels!
5 Upon your race you laid a heavy load;
you slaked us with delirious wine!
6 You raised a banner for your worshipers,
that thus they might escape the enemy's bow;

59:3. *You broke our battle lines:* i.e., you brought it about that our
enemies broke our battle lines.

7 that your belovèd children might be freed,
  now hear us, and give help with your right arm!

II   8 God has spoken in his holy shrine:
  "With joy will I divide up Sichem,
  and parcel out the Succoth vale;
  9 mine is the land of Galaad; mine is Manasses' land;
  the helmet of my head is Ephraim; Juda is my sceptre.
  10 Moab is my washing bowl;
  on Edom will I put my heel,
  and triumph o'er Philistia."

III   11 Who is to lead me to the fortified town,
  who is to escort me as far as Edom?
  12 Not you, O God, who beat us back,
  not you, O God, who now no longer with our armies march?
  13 O give us help against the foe;
  for vain is any help of man.
  14 With God's help we will bravely act;
  and he will trample down our foes.

Psalm 60

The King Prays; He Is Heard; He Exults

I. King David, in exile (cf. 2 Sam. 15–19) asks God to permit him
to return to the Holy City and Mount Sion (2–5). II. His prayers
are heard; he asks for grace and a long life to enjoy this favor (6–9).

59:8–10. The names of the regions or tribes which God has promised
would be made subject to the Israelites are mentioned in these verses. Sichem,
in central Palestine, represents the land west of the Jordan, and Succoth
vale, which is south of the Jabbok River, represents the territory east of
the Jordan. Likewise Galaad and Manasses stand for the land east, and
Ephraim and Juda for the land west of Jordan. Moab, Edom, and Philistia
were hostile countries surrounding Israel. These will be reduced to a state
of slavery.

59:9b. Ephraim, the strongest of all the tribes, is to be like *the helmet*
of his head; Juda will be his *sceptre*, i.e., the seat of his kingdom.

59:10. Moab, a pagan tribe, will be his *washing bowl*, which is used as
a symbol of the humiliation to which they will be subjected.

59:10b. *on Edom will I put my heel*: i.e., as a sign of possession.

59:11. *the fortified town*: probably the town of Petra, which was the
capital of Edom and was strongly fortified and very difficult of access.

PSALM 61 87

¹ *To the choirmaster. For stringed instruments. A psalm of David.*

I ² Hear, Lord, my cry!
List to my prayer!
  ³ From earth's extremity I cry to you,
for sinking is my heart!
O set me on a lofty rock and grant me rest.
  ⁴ My shield you are, a fastness giving shelter from the foe.
  ⁵ Would I could dwell forever in your tent,
find refuge under cover of your wings!

II ⁶ Yes, you have heard my vows, O God;
you gave to me your worshipers' inheritance!
  ⁷ Add days and days to the life of the king,
and may his years keep pace with ages yet to come.
  ⁸ O may his rule be everlasting under God!
Send your own grace and faithfulness to keep him safe.
  ⁹ Thus will I always hymn your name,
and pay my vows day after day.

PSALM 61

In God Alone We Place Our Trust

The main thought of the psalm is expressed in the beginning of the first and second parts; it is repeated in almost the same words in 2, 3; 6, 7. The theme is: God alone is my salvation; I will never be disturbed. I. In contrast to this trust, the psalmist reveals the vain attempts of his foes to ruin him by force and trickery (4, 5). II. He then shows why all hope must be placed in God alone (8, 9). III. Finally, he points out that human power is of no avail, for it is God alone who wields lasting power and justice (10–12).

¹ *To the choirmaster. To the musician, Iduthun. A psalm of David.*

I ² *In God alone my soul finds rest;
from him my safety comes.*
  ³ *Alone he is my rock, my savior,
my guard; and never shall I fall!*

60:3. *From earth's extremity:* in the psalms this phrase almost always means a very distant place. David here uses the phrase figuratively.
60:7. The king asks for a long life for himself (cf. Ps. 20:5).

⁴ How long will you assail a man, how long try, all of you, to
    break him down —
like to a tottering wall or caved-in masonry!
⁵ Yes, from my eminence they plot to hurl me down!
In lying speech they revel:
their lips pronounce a blessing;
their hearts invoke a curse!

II ⁶ *In God alone find rest, my soul;*
from him comes all I hope.
  ⁷ *Alone he is my rock, my savior,*
my guard: I shall not fall!
  ⁸ My safety and my glory rest with God,
my rock and strength: my refuge is in God.
  ⁹ O trust in him, my people, at all times,
and in his sight pour out your hearts.
Our refuge is our God.

III ¹⁰ Poor mortal men — a breath they are, no more!
The great and proud — how they belie their pomp!
Laid in the scales, they mount up high,
and all together weigh less than a breath!
  ¹¹ Confide not in oppression, nor vainly boast of ill-got pelf:
if wealth increases, do not set your heart on it.
  ¹² When God spoke once for all, two things I heard:
"God has power, and you, O Lord, have grace;
to everyone you render according to his deeds."

61:6, 7. The words of vv. 2, 3 are repeated, but here they are addressed
to the psalmist's own soul.
  61:10 ff. *Poor mortal men:* the lowly, nobles, men of great distinction —
these all, placed on the scales at the same time, do not weigh as much as
a breath.
  61:12c. *to everyone you render:* cf. Rom. 2:6–11.

PSALM 62

Longing for God, Our Life and Our Salvation

I. As the dry land longs for water, so the psalmist's soul thirsts for God; he yearns to contemplate him in his holy place and experience his power and graciousness (2–4). II. God, whom he remembers night and day, is his greatest good and it is to him that his soul clings absolutely (5–9). III. The psalmist's foes will perish miserably, but he and his servants will rejoice (10–12).

1 *A psalm of David. This was when he tarried in the desert of Juda.*

I   2 O God, my God you are!
With anxious heart I look for you!
My soul, my flesh — they thirst, they yearn for you,
like dried-up, thirsting, waterless soil.
   3 So in the holy place do I contemplate you
that I may see your glory and your might.
   4 More precious is your graciousness than life;
therefore my lips will hymn your praise.

II   5 So will I bless you in my life,
and in your name uplift my hands.
   6 As I am pleased with rich, delicious food,
so will my lips exult in praising you,
   7 when I remember you upon my couch,
and in my nightly vigils meditate on you.
   8 For, you have proved yourself my help,
and in the shadow of your wings I jubilate!
   9 I cling to you with heart and soul;
your right hand bears me up.

III   10 But those who seek to ruin me
shall sink into the depths of earth.
   11 They shall be given over to the sword;
the prey of jackals they shall be.

62:6. To praise God is more pleasing to the soul of the psalmist than to partake of a sumptuous banquet.
62:11b. *the prey of jackals:* i.e., lacking burial, their bodies shall be devoured by wild beasts.

12 The king, however, shall rejoice in God;
   and glory is for him alone who swears by him.
   Indeed, the mouth of liars shall be stopped!

PSALM 63

God's Judgment on Treacherous Persecutors

I. The psalmist asks God's aid against evil, lying men, those who
oppose good men with double-dealing (2–7). II. For these, he
predicts ruin, and this will be a warning to all and a joy to the
faithful (8–11).

1 To the choirmaster. A psalm of David.

I   2 Hear, God, my plaintive cry;
      from fear of foe preserve my life.
    3 Protect me from the clique of evil men,
      from evildoers' hue and cry.
    4 Like swords, they edge their tongues;
      like shafts, they aim their poisoned words.
    5 They plan to strike from ambush at the innocent,
      to strike him unexpectedly and unafraid.
    6 They firmly are resolved to do an evil deed,
      and secretly conspire to lay their snares;
      they say: "Who will see us, after all?"
    7 They hatch out vicious plans; their hatchings they conceal;
      and each one's heart and mind is an abyss.

II 8 But God smites them with shafts;
      with wounds they are afflicted unexpectedly.
    9 Their own tongue digs their grave;
      and all that see them shake their heads.
   10 And all are struck with fear, and praise the work of God,
      and meditate upon his acts.
   11 The good are joyful in the Lord and confidently turn to him;
      and all the true of heart are jubilant.

62:12b. To swear by God is an act of worship by which his supreme
authority is acknowledged (cf. Deut. 6:13).
63:8, 9. The more clever their schemes are, the closer is their ruin.

PSALM 64

Solemn Thanksgiving for the Blessings of God

I. Thanksgiving for the remission of sin and admission into the temple with all its blessings and graces (2–5). II. Praise of God, the Creator and Lord of nature and of all mankind (6–9). III. Thanksgiving for the fertility of nature and the favor of a rich harvest, which God produced by the blessing of abundant rains (10–14).

1 *To the choirmaster. A psalm of David. A song.*

I   2 A hymn, O God, in Sion is your due;
and let a vow be paid to you,
3 O answerer of prayers!
To you comes all mankind
4 for pardon of its sins.
Our failings weigh us down;
you pardon them.
5 O well for him whom you elect and take in hand:
he has a home within your courts.
may we be sated with the blessings of your house,
your temple's sanctity!

II   6 Stupendous portents you display when you,
our savior God, in mercy hear our prayers.
The hope of the vast wide earth are you,
the hope of distant seas.
7 Your strength makes mountains permanent,
for you are girt with might.
8 You curb the roaring of the sea,
the roaring of its waves, the nations' turbulence.
9 And they who dwell at the world's far edge are by your portents awed;
both farthest east and west, you fill with joy.

III   10 You visited the land and irrigated it;
and wondrously enriched its soil.
God's stream ran full.

64:10c. *God's stream:* i.e., the rainfall which is considered as having its origin in heavenly reservoirs.

You thus prepared the land,
prepared it well to grow the people's grain.
11 You watered well its furrows,
and smoothed its clods;
your showers softened it,
you blessed its fruitfulness.
12 You crowned the year with your beneficence;
your tracks with fatness drip;
13 drip, too, the pastures of the wilderness;
the hillocks gird themselves with jubilee;
14 the meadows clothe themselves with flocks;
the vales are decked with wheat:
they shout and sing for joy!

PSALM 65

A Hymn for a Sacrifice of Thanksgiving

The psalm honors the providence that God has always exercised over
his people. It opens with a proem, in which the whole earth is
called upon to praise God (1–4). I. The people next recall the
blessing of their deliverance from Egypt, then the help which God
gave them in all calamities, even though, at times, he did sorely try
them (5–12). II. For a danger lately overcome, they now fulfill
the vows they had promised; they offer holocausts and praise God,
who so lovingly heard their prayers (13–20).

1 To the choirmaster. A song. A psalm.

O leap for joy in God, all lands!
2 O hymn the glory of his name!
Of choicest praise give him his due,
3 and say to God: "O how stupendous are your works!
Transcendent is your strength: your enemies before you cringe!
4 Let all the earth adore and sing to you,
aye, sing the praises of your name!"

64:12b. *your tracks:* God is conceived of as riding over the earth in a
royal chariot, bestowing benefits as he proceeds.
65:3b. *your enemies before you cringe:* even though they are unwilling
to recognize your greatness, your enemies come cringing before you (cf.
Ps. 17:45; 80:16).

I   5   O come and see the works of God,
      what wondrous things he did for men!
  6   Into arid land he turned the sea;
      dry-shod they crossed the stream.
      Therefore let us rejoice in him!
  7   And by his might he rules eternally;
      his eyes observe the nations:
      let none rebel and rear their heads!
  8   O nations, bless our God;
      and make the world re-echo with his praise!
  9   'Tis he imparted life to us,
      and did not let us stumble on our way.
  10   You, certainly, O God, have tested us,
      tried us by fire as silver is refined.
  11   You led us all into a trap,
      and laid a heavy burden on our backs;
  12   you made men march right o'er our heads;
      through fire and water we have passed;
      but now relief you granted us.

II   13   And I will go into your house with holocausts,
      and pay to you my vows,
  14   vows which my lips pronounced,
      for which, in my distress, I pledged my word.
  15   Holocausts of fattened sheep, wrapt with the fat of rams, will
       I offer you;
      both goats and oxen will I sacrifice.
  16   Come, hear, all worshipers of God, and I will tell
      what great things he has done for me!
  17   'Twas he to whom I loudly cried,
      and then I praised Him with my tongue!
  18   Had I planned evil in my heart,
      the Lord would not have answered me.
  19   But God did answer me;
      he listened to my prayerful cry.
  20   O blest be God, who did not spurn my prayer,
      nor turned away from me his tenderness!

Psalm 66

A Blessing Is Asked Upon the Work of Spreading the Faith Among the Gentiles

This psalm was probably sung in thanksgiving for the harvest. It deals with the responsibility that the Israelites have of bringing to all nations the messianic blessing (cf. Gen. 12:2, 3). This argument is indicated in the refrain, vv. 4, 6. I. The people ask God for the grace of making known salvation to the Gentiles (2, 3). II. Next they invite all nations to praise God's just rule over all peoples (5). III. Finally, then, they ask that God, who has blessed the harvest, will also bless his people in the performance of their higher duty (7, 8).

¹ *To the choirmaster. For stringed instruments. A psalm. A song.*

I   ² May God be merciful to us, and bless us,
     and grant to us the favor of his smile!
   ³ O may the earth have knowledge of his ways,
     and all the nations know his saving grace!
   ⁴ *O may the peoples hymn your praise, O God,*
     O may all peoples hymn your praise!

II   ⁵ O may the nations be in rapturous joy,
     because you rule the peoples with all equity,
     and sway the nations on the earth!
   ⁶ *O may the peoples hymn your praise, O God;*
     O may all the peoples hymn your praise!

III   ⁷ The earth has yielded up its fruit:
     God, our God, has blessed us!
   ⁸ O bless us, God;
     may all the earth do reverence to Him!

PSALM 67

Triumphal Journey of the Ark From Egypt to Mount Sion

In this triumphal song, the journey of the Lord, present above the Ark, from Egypt to Mount Sion, is described. The psalm was probably chanted during the solemn processions with which the Israelites were accustomed to accompany the Ark.

I. The psalm begins with words which were customarily used to indicate the start of a procession of the Ark (cf. Num. 10:35). Before God, present above the Ark, let the enemies flee, the just rejoice (2–4). II. The passage of God through the desert is described (cf. vv. 5, 8). He who passes is the father, the defender, the liberator of the people (5–7). III. The same God manifested himself on Mount Sinai. He benignly provided the people with food, drink, and a fertile land in which to dwell (8–11). IV. There is a brief review of the battles that were fought in taking the land of Chanaan (12–15). V. Mount Sion is chosen as the Lord's dwelling place (16–19). VI. Mention is made of other wars in which God had saved his people (20–24). VII. The procession is described. Tribes other than Israel take part in this holy march (25–28). VIII. God, who now dwells in the sanctuary, is asked that, since the enemies have been vanquished, distant nations may also come to render him tribute (29–32). IX. Finally, all nations are invited to praise the powerful God of Israel (33–36).

1 To the choirmaster. A psalm of David. A song.

I 2 God rises, and his foes are scattered,
   and from his presence all that hate him flee!
  3 As smoke, they vanish;
   as wax melts at the fire, so sinners disappear at God's advance!
  4 But oh, the saints are glad! They leap for joy at sight of God,
   and in their joy they jubilate!

II 5 O sing to God and hymn his name!
   Carpet the way for him who through the desert rides!
   His name is "Lord!"
   And in his sight exult!
  6 The father of the fatherless, protector of the widows,
   is God within his holy dwelling place.

⁷ A home for the abandoned God prepares,
  leads captives to prosperity;
  and none but rebels sojourn in the torrid land.

III ⁸ When you went forth, O God, the vanguard of your people,
     when you went onward through the wilderness,
   ⁹ then shook the earth, the heavens rained, as God advanced;
     then Sinai quaked at sight of God, the God of Israel.
  ¹⁰ Abundant rain you sent, O God, upon your heritage,
     and you refreshed it in its weariness.
  ¹¹ Your flock then settled in the land;
     your goodness had prepared it for the poor, O God.

IV ¹² The Lord gives out the word,
      and mighty is the throng that tells the happy news:
   ¹³ "Kings and their hosts are put to headlong flight;
      the housewives then divide the spoils.
   ¹⁴ While you were resting midst the cattle pens,
      the wings of the dove with silver shone,
      her pinions, with the sheen of gold.
   ¹⁵ While the almighty scattered there the kings,
      Salmon was blanketed with snow."

V ¹⁶ High hills the hills of Basan are,
     steep hills the hills of Basan are:
  ¹⁷ steep hills, why are you looking enviously
     at that one hill where God is pleased to dwell —
     yes, where the Lord will dwell forevermore?

67:7c. *none but rebels:* i.e., those faithless Israelites who did not obey God in the desert (cf. Num. 16).

67:8. *When you went forth:* i.e., in a column of fire and cloud.

67:12. *gives out the word:* victory depends on the Lord; his word decides the battle.

67:12–15. These lines contain a brief review of the battles that were fought with the Gentiles over the possession of the land of Chanaan.

67:13b. The soldiers, returning from the war, bring much booty, which is divided by the housewives.

67:14. This verse probably refers to those tribes of Israel which were absent from the battle (they were *resting*) and occupied themselves with the care of their flocks, while Israel (the *dove*) shone with gold and silver, which, as victor, it had taken from the enemy. The glistening colors of a dove's wings in the sunlight suggested the figure.

67:15b. *Salmon was blanketed with snow:* the soldiers of the enemy fell as numerous as flakes of snow.

¹⁸ A myriad are the chariots of God, a thousand and a thousand
    more;
from Sinai comes the Lord into his holy place.
¹⁹ You mounted up on high, led captives in your train:
and human beings in tribute you received;
yes, even such as do not wish to live with the Lord God!

VI ²⁰ Blest be the Lord day in, day out;
    our Savior God our burden bears.
    ²¹ Our God is the God who saves;
    the Lord God grants escape from death.
    ²² In truth, God breaks his enemies' heads,
    the hairy pate of him who lives in sin.
    ²³ The Lord has said: "From Basan will I bring them back,
    back even from the depths of the sea,
    ²⁴ that you may dip your foot in gore,
    and that your dogs may munch away at enemy flesh."

VII ²⁵ They watch your entry, God,
    the entry of my God, my King, into the holy place.
    ²⁶ The choirmasters are the van, the minstrels form the rear;
    between them maidens play the tambourine:
    ²⁷ "Bless God in festive gatherings;
    bless God, you sons of Israel."
    ²⁸ There is the youngest, Benjamin, preceding all;
    the princes of Juda with their bands,
    the princes of Zabulon, the princes of Nephthalim.

VIII ²⁹ Exert, O God, your might,
    your might, O God, who act on our behalf.
    ³⁰ Because your shrine is in Jerusalem,
    bid kings to offer gifts to you.
    ³¹ Rebuke the jungle beast —

67:19. After the victory had been won, the Ark of the Covenant, which
had been taken with the expedition, is brought back to Mount Sion, together with the captives that had been taken.
  67:22b. *hairy pate*: the enemies were terrifying in their barbaric appearance.
  67:23. *From Basan*: i.e., from high mountains as in contrast with the
depths of the sea in the next line.
  67:24. *that you may dip your foot in gore*: cf. Ps. 57:11.
  67:31. *the jungle beast*: i.e., the Egyptians, whose symbol was the crocodile,
which infested the swamps of the Nile (cf. v. 32).

the troop of steers with all their subject herds.
Let them kneel down, enriched with silver coin;
stampede the tribes whose joy is war.
32 May potentates from Egypt come,
and Ethiopia stretch its hands to God.

IX 33 Sing, kingdoms of the earth, to God; make music to the Lord,
34 who rides across the skies, those immemorial skies!
Mark well, he sounds his voice, a mighty voice:
35 "Confess the might of God!"
Over Israel broods his majesty;
his might is in the clouds.
36 Awful is God within his holy place, the God of Israel;
'tis he grants to his people might and strength.
O blest be God!

Psalm 68

Prayer of a Man Who Is Grievously Afflicted for the Sake of God

I. The psalmist describes his affliction figuratively (2–5). II. He suffers this persecution, not because he deserves it, but rather because of his fidelity to God (6–13). III. Hence, he urgently asks God that he might be freed from his troubles (14–22). IV. For his wicked persecutors, he seeks a just punishment (23–29). V. He promises thanksgiving (30–33). There follows an exhortation to the Israelites in exile in Babylon, who are looking forward to the restoration of the city of Jerusalem and the Kingdom of Juda (34–37).

1 To the choirmaster. To the melody, "The Lilies." A psalm of David.

I 2 Save me, O God,
for the waters are rising to my neck.
3 Immersed I am in abysmal mire;
I have no ground to set my foot upon;
1 am in water far beyond my depth,
and the flood is drowning me.

67:31b. the troop of steers: i.e., the leaders of the people, whom the latter follow like cattle.

4 Worn out I am with shouting;
by now my throat is hoarse;
my eyes have lost their sight
while I look for help from my God.

5 More numerous than the hairs of my head
are those who hate me unprovoked;
in strength, I am no match
for those who fiercely combat me.
Must I restore the goods I did not steal?

II   6 O God, you know my foolishness;
to you no secret are my sins.

7 Do not, on my account, let those be shamed whose hope you are,
Lord, Lord of hosts.
Let not, on my account, your worshipers be put to shame, O
God of Israel.

8 For your sake, surely, I am meeting with reproach,
confusion mantles on my face.

9 A stranger to my brethren am I now,
an alien to my mother's sons.

10 Zeal for your house has ruined me;
reproaches aimed at you have buried me.

11 I have inflicted fasts upon myself;
they, too, turned out to my reproach.

12 The sackcloth was my daily garb;
and I became their laughingstock.

13 The gossips at the gate find fault with me;
the tavern haunters carp at me.

III   14 But I direct my prayer to you, O Lord.
O let this be a day of grace, O God.
Hear me because your kindness knows no bounds,
because your help will never fail.

15 Save me from sinking in the mire;
from such as hate me, rescue me,
and from a watery grave.

16 Let not the surging waters bury me;
let not the whirlpool suck me down;

68:5e. *Must I restore the goods I did not steal?* This was probably a
proverbial expression to indicate one's complete innocence.

let not the pit's mouth close on me.
17 Hear me, O Lord; you are so kind, so merciful!
In your abounding tenderness, look down on me;
18 and from your servant do not hide your face.
I am in trouble: quickly answer me.
19 Come close to me; deliver me;
despite my enemies set me free.
20 You know my shame, disgrace, reproach;
well-known to you are all that trouble me.
21 Heartbroken with disgrace, I faint away;
I looked for one to pity me: but none there was;
for one to comfort me: but none I found.
22 And with my food they mingled gall,
and in my thirst they gave me vinegar to drink.

IV 23 May their own table be a snare for them,
and for their friends a trap.
24 And may their eyes grow dim and blind,
their limbs be ever limp and loose.
25 Pour out on them the vials of your wrath;
the fury of your anger seize on them.
26 Their homes be turned to wastes,
their tents be uninhabited,
27 because they persecute him whom you smote;
the pain of him you wounded they increase.
28 Add to their debit, guilt on guilt;
do not declare them quit and clear of guilt.
29 May they be blotted from the book of life,
and not be listed with the saints.

V 30 But I am wretched and in pain.
O may your help, God, shelter me.
31 Then I will praise God's name with song,
and with thanksgiving hymn his praise.

68:23. The oriental table was a cushion or rug spread out on the floor, in which the foot could easily be caught, thus causing one to fall.

68:23–28. The psalmist calls down on his enemies punishments which were due to them according to the just judgments of God; this was the standard, according to the law of retribution (the *lex talionis*), which obtained in the Old Testament (cf. v. 27).

[32] And this will please God more than steer
or bullock horned and hoofed.
[33] Look, humble souls; rejoice;
you look for God: then may your hearts revive.
[34] The Lord gives audience to the poor;
his saints in chains he does not scorn.
[35] Let heaven and earth his praises sing,
the seas and all that moves about in them.
[36] For God will rescue Sion Hill,
build Juda's principalities:
and they will dwell there and possess the land.
[37] The offspring of his servants will inherit it;
and those who love his name shall dwell in it.

PSALM 69

A Petition for Divine Help

This psalm, with a few minor changes, is the same as Ps. 39:14–18.
It is probably separated from the earlier one because it forms in
itself a beautiful petition for divine aid.

[1] *To the choirmaster. A psalm of David. For a commemoration.*

[2] O may it please you, God, to rescue me;
make haste to help me, Lord.
[3] Let those be shamed and blush
who seek my life;
let those be put to shame and driven back
who gloat upon my miseries.
[4] Let those be routed and discomfited
who say to me: "Ha! Ha!"
[5] May those rejoice in you with jubilant hearts
who look to you for help.
May those who hunger for your help
say constantly: "May God be glorified!"
[6] For me, I am a wretched man and poor;
O God, come to my aid!
You are my helper, my deliverer;
O Lord, do not delay!

Psalm 70

"Do Not Discard Me in My Age"

The author of the psalm is a good man now grown old (vv. 9, 18), and who is suffering persecution (vv. 4, 10, 11, 24). I. A pious old man seeks aid from God, who has protected him from his infancy, in whom he always put his trust, and whom he always praised (1–8). II. He describes the plans of his foes, and from God, to whom he will always be grateful, he seeks assistance (9–16). III. Mindful of the help of God, which he had experienced in all the difficulties of life, he now asks that he may have his help in his old age; he promises gratitude for this blessing, too (17–24).

I   1 To you, O Lord, I confidently fly:
let me not be forever put to shame!
2 In your justice rescue and deliver me;
incline your ear to me: save me!
3 O be to me a rock of refuge and a citadel, and thus save me:
in truth, my rock, my citadel are you!

4 My God, save me from a sinner's grip;
and from a vile oppressor's clutch.
5 You are my expectation, O my God;
O Lord, you are my hope from childhood up!
6 On you I have been leaning from my birth;
from my mother's womb, you have protected me;
and I have always hoped in you!
7 As 'twere a prodigy I have appeared to many
because my mighty helper you have been.
8 Rich praise my lips have given you;
the livelong day your glory was my theme.

II   9 Do not discard me in my age;
and when my strength is on the wane, do not abandon me.
10 For I have enemies that speak of me;
they watch me and conspire.

70:7. a prodigy: because, though he had been afflicted with so many calamities in life, he was always aided by God.

11 They say: "God has abandoned him!
Pursue him and lay hold of him!
There is no one to rescue him."

12 God, do not stand aloof from me;
my God, make haste to bring me help!

13 Let those who plot against my life be shamed and foiled;
let those who seek to do me harm be clothed in utter shame.

14 But I will always hope,
each day I will contribute to your highest praise.

15 The livelong day my lips shall blaze your justice, and the help
you have bestowed;
for they are past my numbering.

16 I will rehearse God's might
and will proclaim, O Lord, your justice; for it has no peer.

III 17 O God, you schooled me from my youth,
and even now I still proclaim your wondrous deeds.

18 Now, too, when I am old and grey of hair,
O God, do not abandon me
till I proclaim to this and all the coming generations that mighty
arm of yours,

19 your justice too, O God, which reaches to the skies,
which made you do such wondrous things! O God, who is
your peer?

20 Full many grievous trials you laid on me;
O quicken me again and lift me from the depths of earth.

21 Make me respected once again,
and once more comfort me.

22 And I in turn will hymn with psalmody your faithfulness,
and praise you with the harp, O Holy One of Israel.

23 With jubilee my lips shall sing a song to you;
so shall my soul, which you restored to life.

24 Your justice, too, my tongue shall hymn the livelong day:
for all who plot my fall have blushed and are discomfited.

70:21. *Make me respected once again:* by freeing me from the afflictions
that now bear down upon me.

70:22b. *Holy One of Israel:* God is only given this title in the Old Testament to emphasize his sanctity and the special relationship by which the
people of Israel were bound to him.

Psalm 71

The Messianic Kingdom

According to both the Jewish and Christian tradition, this psalm refers to the Messias and his reign. The psalm attributes to this reign perpetual duration (5–7) and universal extension (8–11, 17). The praise of the Messias is sung in the following five sections: I: as just and beneficent (1–4); II: as eternal (5–7); III: as universal (8–11); IV: as benign toward the humble and afflicted (12–14); V: as prosperous and glorious forever (15–17). Verses 18, 19 are a doxology which concludes Book II of the Psalms.

1 *A psalm of Solomon.*

I   O God, confer your judgment on the king,
your justice, on the royal heir:
2 bid him with justice rule your chosen race,
with equity, your humble worshipers.
3 Then will the mountains burgeon peace upon the people,
the hills bring justice forth.
4 He will be warden of the humble folk,
and save the children of the poor,
and trample the oppressor under foot.

II 5 Long as the sun lasts, he will live;
long as the moon, from age to age.
6 He will be like the rain distilling on the grass,
like showers that irrigate the earth.
7 Justice will flourish in his time,
a plenitude of peace until the moon gives out.

III 8 He will be Lord from sea to sea,
and from the river to the outmost lands.

71:1b. *royal heir:* the Messias is himself the king and he is descended from a royal line.

71:3. *the mountains . . . the hills:* i.e., the whole region inhabited by his people.

71:8. He will be Lord from the western (Mediterranean) sea to the eastern (the Persian Gulf) sea, and from the river (the Euphrates) to the outmost lands (the islands and lands of the farthest west). Therefore, he will be Lord of the whole world.

9 His enemies will pay him homage,
  his foes will lick the dust.
10 The kings of Tharsis and the Isles will offer gifts,
  Arabia's and Saba's kings will bring their offerings.
11 All kings will worship him,
  all nations be his thralls.

IV 12 For he will free the poor man seeking him,
  the wretched one, bereft of help.
13 He will be merciful to poor and helpless souls,
  and save the poor men's lives:
14 from wrong and from oppression he will rescue them;
  and precious in his sight will be their blood.

V 15 And therefore he will live, and gold from Arabia will be given him,
  and prayers for him will mount unceasingly,
  and blessing after blessing be invoked on him.
16 Of wheat there will be plenty in the land;
  on mountain tops its crops will rustle like the woods of Lebanon;
  the citizens will bloom like grass upon the leas.
17 And blest will be his name forevermore;
  his name will last as long as sun will shine;
  all tribes upon the earth will find in him their blessedness;
  all nations will acclaim him "Blest!"

18 Blest be the Lord, the God of Israel,
  who has no peer in doing wondrous things;
19 blest be his glorious name eternally;
  and with his glory all the earth shall be replete.
  So be it! Be it so!

71:9b. *lick the dust:* a semitic expression which indicates total subjection.
71:10. *Tharsis and the Isles:* i.e., the kings of Tartessus in South Spain
(cf. Ps. 47:8), and the islands and shores of the Mediterranean; *Arabia's
and Saba's kings,* whose territories abounded in gold.
71:14b. *their blood:* i.e., their life; he will not permit the blood of the
innocent to be shed (cf. Ps. 115:15).
71:18, 19. This is the doxology with which the second book of the
psalms ends; these verses do not pertain to the psalm itself. Cf. Ps. 40:14.

BOOK 3: Psalms 72-88

PSALM 72

Problem of the Prosperity of the Wicked and Its Solution

This beautiful psalm deals, as do Psalms 36 and 48, with the question of how the justice of God can be reconciled with the fact that the wicked are prosperous and happy. The answer given here is more satisfactory and profound than that given in those earlier psalms. It is to the effect that life does not end man's lot, but that there is an afterlife in which the wicked will perish and the good enjoy God.

The psalmist states that because of the happiness of the wicked, his trust in God had wavered (1–3). I. He pictures the lot of the wicked (4–12); they are happy and proud (4–9); they wield destructive authority over the people (10–12). II. He next tells of his own internal strife and the exhausting effect of trying to find a solution to this problem by his own efforts; the solution, ultimately, is given to him by a divine illumination (13–17). III. He here shows what is the final end of the wicked: they are as transitory as the dream of a sleeper. If a man does not understand this, he is a fool (18–22). IV. The just man, on the contrary, is taken care of by God, who wisely directs him, and, at the end, takes him up into glory, where God himself, the greatest and only good, will be his portion forever (23–28).

1 A *psalm* of *Asaph*.

How good is the Lord to the true of heart!
How good is the Lord to single-minded men!
2 And yet, my feet came close to faltering,
my steps had almost slipped!
3 Yes, I was jealous of the wicked mob
as I the sinners' prosperous lot observed.

I   4 No torment ever touches them!
How sound and sleek their bodies are!
5 From mortals' pangs they are exempt;
they are not scourged like other men!
6 Pride, like a necklace, clasps them round,
and like a mantle violence covers them!

72:6. Pride and violence are their garments and ornaments.

109

7 The grossness of their hearts exudes iniquity;
all their caprices blossom into acts.
8 They jeer and talk maliciously;
and, throned on high, they threaten tyranny!
9 Their lips indulge in blasphemy;
their censure spares no man on earth!
10 Alas, my people follow them,
and draughts of water they gulp down!
11 They say: "How, after all, is God aware of this?
Does any knowledge come to the Most High?"
12 You see, such is the brood of wicked men;
and, always tranquil, they enhance their might!

II 13 Have I in vain, then, kept my purity of heart,
and washed my hands among the innocent?
14 I suffer scourges all the while;
my daily lot is chastisement.
15 If I should think: "I'll speak like these,"
I should turn traitor to your race.
16 So I bethought myself to solve this riddle,
and oh, how difficult it seemed to me —
17 until I pierced the holy mind of God
and meditated on the sinners' end.

III 18 Indeed, you place them on a slippery path;
you hurl them into ruinous depths.
19 How suddenly they have collapsed
and disappeared, a prey to frightful fear!
20 Just like a dream when one awakes, O Lord,
so will you shatter their mirage when you arise.
21 Oh, when my mind gave way to bitter thoughts
and when my heart was piqued,
22 I was a fool and did not understand;
and in your eyes I was a senseless brute.

72:10. The verse means that the Israelites, following the bad example of these haughty sinners, indulge in pleasures of no value: *draughts of water*.

72:11. *They say*: it is the plain, simple people who have been led astray who are speaking here.

72:15. The psalmist wants to remain faithful to the tradition of the chosen people.

72:20. When the Lord arises to judge these men, he will shatter their false notions as quickly as a mirage, on desert or sea, might be dissipated.

IV 23 But I shall always be with you;
        for you have taken hold of my right hand.
    24 And by your counsel you will lead me on
        and take me up to glory in the end.
    25 What else is there in heaven for me but you?
        And, if I am with you, the earth has no delights for me.
    26 My flesh is wasting, wasting is my heart:
        the firm rock of my heart, my portion, is God eternally!
    27 Alas, those who depart from you are doomed;
        you ruin all who break their faith with you.
    28 For me, how good it is to be near God,
        to make the Lord, my God, my safe retreat!
        And I will tell the tale of all your deeds
        at Sion's well-loved city-gates!

PSALM 73

Lamentation and Prayers Over the Devastated Temple

The temple had been burned by the Chaldeans in 587 B.C. I. The
psalmist describes the havoc and profanation committed in the
temple by the enemy, and he beseeches God to have mercy on his
people (1–11). II. Meditating devoutly on the wonderful things
that God had done in creating the world (12–17), he now asks for
help from this same God, whose part it is, he says, to further his
own cause (18–23).

    1 A *maskil* of Asaph.

I   Why have you, God, made your rejection permanent?
        Why does your anger flare against the sheep of your own
        pasturing?
    2   Remember your community — you founded it of old;
        your tribe — you ransomed it to be your own;
        your Sion Hill — 'tis there you fixed your residence!
    3   Direct your steps to where the loss is irretrievable:
        the foe has turned the holy place into a total wreck!
    4   Your enemies now roar where once your people met,
        and raise their ensigns to proclaim their victory.
    5   Like woodmen in a copse, they swing their axe,

72:25, 26. Compared with the supreme good, all earthly goods are as
nothing; the supreme good is to be near God (v. 28).

⁶ and now with hatchet and with hammer smash its gates.
⁷ They made your holy place a prey to fire,
and sullied in the dust the tabernacle of your name.
⁸ And to themselves they said: "Let us make havoc of them all!
Burn down all shrines of God on earth!"
⁹ The signs once granted us we see no more; no prophet is at hand;
not one among us knows how long this is to last.
¹⁰ How long, God, shall the enemy revile?
And shall the foe blaspheme your name eternally?
¹¹ Why, then, do you withdraw your hand,
why keep your right hand in your bosom hid?

II ¹² But God has been my king from olden times;
he is the source of blessings in the land.
¹³ 'Tis you who blasted by your might the sea,
and in the waters crushed the dragons' heads.
¹⁴ You crushed Leviathan's head,
and gave him up as food to monsters of the sea.
¹⁵ You drew forth springs and torrents;
you dried up swollen streams.
¹⁶ Yours is the day, and yours the night;
to moon and sun you gave a steady course.
¹⁷ You fixed the boundaries of every land;
and you arranged the summer and the winter shifts.

¹⁸ Remember this: the enemy has reviled you, Lord;
a foolish people cursed your name.
¹⁹ Do not betray to vultures your dear turtle dove;
do not forget forever your dear poor.
²⁰ O look upon your covenant:
the hidden corners of the land, the open fields, are haunts of
violence.
²¹ Let not the humble man go home discomfited;
but may the poor and helpless praise your name.

73:9. *The signs:* i.e., the miracles once worked by God for the Chosen People.

73:13–15. The reference here is to the Exodus. The dragons and Leviathan are the Egyptians who were killed in the Red Sea. Such monsters symbolized the Egyptians.

73:19. *to vultures:* i.e., to fierce enemies. *your dear turtle dove:* i.e., the people of Israel.

22 Rise, God; defend your cause;
    think of the insults which the foolish daily hurl at you.
23 Do not forget the tauntings of your enemies;
    the tumult of your rebel foes mounts up unceasingly.

PSALM 74

The Lord Is a Just Judge

In I (v. 2) and in III (vv. 10, 11), the psalmist is speaking. He sings the praises of God and his works. In II (3–9), God himself speaks, announcing that he, in his own good time, will pass judgment (v. 3), and that he, sole judge (4–8a), decides according to the merit of each individual (8b–9).

1 *To the choirmaster. To the melody, "Do not Destroy." A psalm of Asaph. A song.*

I   2 We joyfully hymn your praise, O Lord;
        we glorify your name; we blaze your wondrous deeds.

II   3 "When I have set the time,
        then will I justly judge.
     4 And should the earth with its inhabitants be out of joint,
        yet have I made its pillars firm and strong.
     5 And to the proud I say: 'Do not be proud';
        and to the godless, 'Do not vaunt your strength!'
     6 No, do not vaunt your strength and challenge the Most High;
        and hurl not insolent speech at God.
     7 Not from the east nor from the west,
        from desert nor from mountain range —
     8 no, no; God is the judge:
        he puts down one, another he exalts.
     9 For in the hand of the Lord there is a cup,
        which foams with wine, with spices drugged:

74:7. In reading this verse add, "comes judgment."
74:9. A cupful of a bitter draught is often used as a symbol of divine wrath. The meaning of this verse is: God is shown as giving the Gentiles the cup of his wrath to drink. It is foaming and brimming over with a potent wine, made more potent by the addition of certain spices. This cup they must drink to the dregs. The draught will make them powerless. Thus they will experience the bitterness of God's anger.

from this he drinks a toast, and they shall gulp it down, dregs
  and all;
and all the wicked on the earth shall drink!"

III   **10**   But I — I will exult eternally;
  to the harp will I sing to Jacob's God.

    11 And all the strength of sinners will I break;
  the good will be made strong.

PSALM 75

Triumphal Song After a Great Victory

The psalm seems to have been composed after a fierce slaughter
inflicted by God on an enemy people, possibly on the Aremai and
Edomites (cf. vv. 11–13), or the forces of King Sennacherib (cf.
Pss. 45, 47; 4 Kings 19).
    I. The psalmist summarily states the fact of the rout (2–4). II. He
tells how the enemy, breathless from fear, were cut to pieces (5–7).
III. He shows that this victory must be attributed to God, who is
powerful and just (8–10). IV. Finally, he calls upon the neighboring
peoples to honor this mighty God of Israel and to offer sacrifices
to him (11–13).

  1 *To the choirmaster. For stringed instruments. A psalm of Asaph.
  A song.*

I   **2** Well-known is God in Juda;
  in Israel his name is great.

    3 In Salem is his holy shrine,
  in Sion is his dwelling place.

    4 'Tis there he shattered the fiery darts,
  the buckler, sword, and tools of war.

II   **5** Splendent with light, you came, O mighty One,
  from the eternal hills:

    6 despoiled were all the stout of heart!
  They sleep their sleep,
  and all the strong men's hands have failed!

75:3. *Salem:* another name for Jerusalem.
   75:5b. *eternal hills:* probably the mountains about Jerusalem (cf. Ps. 23:7);
God appears coming forth from the temple (cf. v. 3).

7 Because of your rebuke, O Jacob's God,
both chariot and horse are numbed.

III   8 Dreadful you are: who can resist you —
for violent is your wrath?
9 From heaven you made your judgment heard;
earth was aghast — yes, it was still —
10 when God arose to act as judge
and save all humble souls throughout the land.

IV 11 Yes, Edom's fury shall extol your glory;
Emath's survivors holiday shall keep to honor you.
12 Make vows, all you, and pay them to the Lord your God;
let all the dwellers round about him bring
their gifts to him, the dreadful One;
13 to Him who curbs the spirit of the great,
who terrifies earth's kings.

PSALM 76

The People Are Afflicted;
Their Consolation, Their Solace

I. The psalmist, even in the midst of his prayers, can find no consolation; the providence of God, he thinks, is changed toward his people (2–13). II. Nevertheless, strength comes to his soul, when he meditates on God's sanctity and power — that power which was shown particularly by the deliverance of the Jewish people from Egypt and the miracles worked at the crossing of the Red Sea (14–21).

1 To the choirmaster. To the musician, Iduthun. A psalm of Asaph.

I   2 My voice mounts up to God, and I cry out;
my voice mounts up to God that he may answer me.
3 In this my day of need I seek the Lord;
my hand by night is lifted up; it never tires;
my soul refuses to be comforted.

75:7. At a mere word from God, men, chariots, and horses are stricken motionless.
75:11. *Edom*, a region southeast of Palestine, and *Emath*, a city in north-central Syria, both are called upon to honor the true God (cf. v. 12).

4 When I remember God, I groan;
  when I take thought, my spirit faints.
5 You keep my eyes awake;
  in my bewilderment I cannot speak.
6 I ponder on the days of old,
  and long-departed years I call to mind.
7 I meditate by night, deep in my heart;
  my spirit ruminates inquiringly:
8 "Will God make his rejection permanent,
  and will not he be gracious once again?
9 His kindness — will it cease forevermore?
  His promise — is it null for good and all?
10 Has God forgotten to be merciful
  or in his anger stemmed his mercy's tide?"
11 And then I say: "This is my grief:
  no more the Most High's hand is what it was!"
12 And I remember what the Lord had done;
  yes, I recall your wondrous deeds of olden times.
13 I meditate on all your works;
  I ponder your accomplishments.

II 14 God, holy is your way!
  What god is great as is our God?
15 You are a God performing wondrous deeds;
  among the nations you revealed your might.
16 Your arm redeemed your chosen race,
  Jacob's and Joseph's sons.
17 The waters saw you, God,
  the waters saw you; and they trembled;
  yes, in a turmoil were the waves.
18 The clouds poured water in abundance;
  the clouds sent forth a roll —
  withal, your arrows flew.
19 Your thunder pealed in a whirl of wind,
  and lightnings lit up all the world;
  the earth quaked and trembled.

76:16b. Jacob's sons were those who had migrated to Egypt; Joseph's sons were those Israelites who had been born there. Cf. Gen. 46:26 ff.

76:17–20. God's intervention at the crossing of the Rea Sea is described after the manner of a splendid theophany (cf. Ps. 17:11–16). God's appearance is accompanied by an upheaval of nature.

20 Across the sea a way was paved;
    your path — it lay through billowing waves,
    yet were your steps not seen.
21 You led your people like a flock
    by Moses' and by Aaron's hand.

PSALM 77

The Blessings of God;
the Ingratitude of the People of Israel

This psalm, like Psalms 104 and 106, deals with the history of the
people of Israel; the psalmist wants the Israelites to learn from their
past errors. This purpose is indicated in the poem (1–8). In the
six following sections, he recounts how great were the blessings of
God and how ungrateful were the people. I. God works miracles in
Egypt and at the Red Sea; he assists the people with a column of
cloud and a pillar of fire; he draws water from a stone (9–16).
II. When the people, not contented, murmur, he sends them manna
and winged fowl for their food, but, at the same time, he chastises
their cupidity (17–31). III. Again and again, the Israelites experience the mercy of God, but unappreciative, they continue to sin
(32–39). IV. The psalmist recalls the miracles worked in Egypt,
the journey through the desert, and that last great blessing by which
God permitted them to take possession of the land of Chanaan (40–
55). V. But in Chanaan, too, they sin against God with their lofty
temples and idols; hence, he punishes them again by disasters inflicted by the Philistines (56–64). VI. At last, God, although he
gave them victory over the enemies, spurns the sanctuary erected
in the city of Silo, rejects the tribe of Ephraim, chooses the tribe of
Juda and Mount Sion, appoints David king (65–72).

1 A maskil of Asaph.

   O hear, my people, what I teach;
   incline your ears to the words I speak.
2 Things fraught with meaning will I lay bare,
   and tell the hidden lessons taught by ancient days.
3 What we have heard and learned —
   the things our fathers told to us —

76:20c. *were your steps not seen:* the apparition of God was not visible
to human eyes. So now God, though unseen, leads his people.

4 we shall not hide from their posterity.
No, we will tell the future race
the praises of the Lord and all his might,
the wondrous things that he has done.
5 For he laid down a rule in Jacob,
and made a law in Israel:
what he enjoined upon our ancestors
they shall make known to their posterity;
6 the coming generation, the sons yet to be born, must know
and must bestir themselves to say to their posterity:
7 "Put your trust in God!
Do not forget the works of God!
Observe whatever he enjoined!
8 No, do not, like your fathers,
become a stubborn and rebellious race,
a race which was not true of heart,
whose spirit was not faithful to their God!"

I 9 The sons of Ephraim, those wielders of the bow,
were routed in the day of battle.
10 They did not keep God's covenant;
and they refused to walk the ways his law enjoined.
11 Ah, they forgot what he had done,
the wonders he had shown to them!
12 Their fathers saw the miracles he wrought
in Egypt's land, on Tanis' plain!
13 The sea he parted and led them across,
and dammed the waters rampartlike.
14 He led them with a cloud by day,
with blazing fire all through the night.
15 He split the rocks in the wilderness,
and gave them water copiously, as from floods;
16 yes, he drew rivers from the rock,
and channelled the water just like streams.

77:9. Ephraim was a very large and powerful tribe, but lacking in strong faith toward God. Although they were expert bowmen, nevertheless they were routed in the day of battle.
77:12b. Tanis: a city of lower Egypt, situated in the Nile delta. It was, at that time, the capital of the kingdom.

II ¹⁷ But they went on to sin against him,
and to offend the Most High in the wilderness;
¹⁸ for in their hearts they tempted God,
demanding food to sate their gluttonness.
¹⁹ They challenged God and said:
"Can God spread us a table in the wilderness?
²⁰ You see, he struck the rock, and water flowed, and streams
gushed forth:
can he give bread as well, or to his people furnish meat?"
²¹ So, when the Lord heard this, his anger flamed;
and fire blazed forth to punish Jacob,
and anger boiled to punish Israel —
²² for they did not believe in God,
nor did they hope for help from him.
²³ But he gave orders to the clouds above,
and opened heaven's sluice,
²⁴ rained manna down for them to eat,
and gave them heaven's bread.
²⁵ Man ate a bread that makes men strong;
he sent them food to glut their appetite.
²⁶ He called the east wind from the sky,
and commandeered the southern blast.
²⁷ He rained down meat on them — like dust,
and winged fowls — like sand upon the beach,
²⁸ which lighted on their camp
and dropped about their tents.
²⁹ And they fell to and gorged themselves.
Thus he complied with their desire.
³⁰ Ere they had ceased from glutting their desire,
while yet their mouths munched on their food,
³¹ God's anger boiled to punish them:
he made a carnage of their strongest men,
and laid the flower of Israel low.

III ³² But yet they sinned still more,
and paid no heed to all his miracles.
³³ And quickly he consumed their days,

77:27. *like dust . . . like sand:* poetical exaggerations to indicate the great
abundance of the food provided.

and brought their years abruptly to an end.
34 While he was slaying them, they looked for him:
they changed their ways and searched for God;
35 and they remembered that their rock was God,
and the Most High God their deliverer.
36 Yet they deceived him with their mouth;
and with their tongue they lied to him!
37 Their heart — it was not true to him;
they were not loyal to his covenant!
38 But, taking pity, he forgave their guilt and did not ruin them;
he checked his anger frequently,
and did not empty all his wrath on them.
39 No, he remembered they were flesh —
a breath that passes and returns no more.

IV 40 How often they provoked him in the wilderness!
How oft they grieved him in the solitude!
41 Again they tempted God,
and irritated Israel's Holy One.
42 Unmindful were they of the might he showed
the day he saved them from their foe;
43 when he in Egypt wrought his miracles,
his portents on the Tanis plain,
44 and turned their rivers into blood —
their streams — so that they could not drink.
45 He sent them flies to devastate their ranks,
and frogs to pester them;
46 their crops — he gave them over to the grasshopper,
and to the locust all their labor's fruit.
47 With hail he struck their vines,
their sycamores with frost.
48 He gave their beasts of burden over to the hail,
their flocks to thunder bolts.
49 He poured on them the caldron of his wrath —
his indignation, rage, and trials all —
a horde of angels of calamity.

77:44–51. The plagues of Egypt are enumerated here, though the order given differs somewhat from that in Exod. 7–12.

77:49c. *angels of calamity*: the afflictions just mentioned are thus personified.

50 And to his ire he gave free scope:
he did not spare their lives,
and gave their cattle over to the plague.

51 He slew in Egypt every first-born thing,
their first-born in the tents of Cham.

52 He led his people out like sheep,
and in the desert, like a flock, escorted them.

53 He led them safely — and they had no fear!
The sea engulfed their foes.

54 He led them on into his holy land,
into the mountain region which his right arm won.

55 To give them room he drove the heathens out,
by lot assigned the lands as heritage,
and settled in their tents the tribes of Israel.

V 56 Alas, they tempted and provoked the Most High God,
and did not keep his laws.

57 And they relaxed and, like their sires, broke faith,
and strayed like a deceitful bow.

58 They stirred his anger by their mountain fanes,
and by their idols roused his jealousy.

59 God knew it, and he boiled with rage,
and, in embitterment, discarded Israel.

60 He turned his back upon his Silo home,
the tent where he had dwelt 'mongst men.

61 And he resigned his stronghold to captivity,
his glory to the hands of enemies.

62 He gave his people over to the sword,
and was enraged against his heritage.

63 Then fire devoured their youth;
their maidens were not wed;

64 their priests fell by the sword;
their widows did not mourn.

VI 65 Then woke the Lord as out of sleep,
like warrior flushed with wine;

77:61. *stronghold . . . glory*: i.e., the Ark of the Covenant.
77:65. *as out of sleep . . . flushed with wine*: these bold figures indicate that God, who before seems to be neglecting his people, now suddenly comes to their defense.

66 he struck the enemies in the rear,
   inflicting on them everlasting shame.
67 And he discarded Joseph's tent,
   and Ephraim's tribe no longer was his choice;
68 no, he chose Juda's tribe —
   the Mount of Sion which he loved.
69 And there he built his shrine, sky-high,
   firm as the earth, which he created for eternity.
70 He chose his servant David,
   and took him from the folds of sheep;
71 he called him from the care of ewes
   to shepherd Jacob, his own race,
   and Israel, his heritage.
72 He tended these with upright heart,
   and guided them with prudent hand.

PSALM 78

Lamentation Over the Destruction of Jerusalem

I. The psalmist grieves over the sad lot of Jerusalem and the temple,
the slaughter of the faithful, the contempt that the neighboring
tribes have for the Israelites (1–4). II. He seeks punishment for these
neighbors and forgiveness for his own people (5–8). III. The very
glory of the name of God requires that aid be given to his people
(9, 10). IV. The psalmist begs God's aid; he promises perpetual
thanksgiving (11–13).

1 A psalm of Asaph.

I   O God, the Gentiles have invaded your inheritance;
   they have defiled your holy shrine;
   they have laid waste Jerusalem!
2 They gave your servants' limbs as food to carrion birds;
   the bodies of your saints to roving beasts!
3 They spilt their blood like water round about Jerusalem;

77:67, 68. The Ark was not returned to Silo, which is situated in
Ephraim. Its sanctuary was established on Mount Sion, among the tribe
of Juda.
78:2, 3. The bodies of the dead were not buried.

and there was none to bury them!
4 We have become a byword to our neighbors,
   the scorn and laughing stock of neighboring tribes!

II 5 How long, O Lord? Will you be wroth eternally?
      How long, like a fire, will your anger flame?
   6 Pour out your wrath on nations not acknowledging you,
      on realms that do not call upon your name!
   7 Indeed, Jacob they have devoured,
      laid waste the land in which he dwells!
   8 Do not, against us, keep a record of our fathers' guilt;
      may your compassion quickly come to us,
      for we are sunk in misery!

III 9 O help us, God, our savior, for the glory of your name;
       deliver us, forgive our sins, in honor of your name!
   10 Why should the Gentiles say:
      "Where is their God?"
      The vengeance for your servants' blood that has been shed —
      let it be known among the Gentiles, in our sight!

IV 11 The groans of the captives reach your ear!
      Your mighty arms release those doomed to death!
   12 Make our neighbors pay, in person, sevenfold,
      for the reproach they brought on you, O Lord!
   13 But we, your race, your pasture's flock —
      we will extol you in eternity,
      from age to age proclaim your praise.

PSALM 79

"Protect the Vine"

I. Great calamity had come to the northern kingdom; the psalmist
seeks the help of God, the shepherd of his people and the leader
of Joseph, for these northern tribes (2, 3). II. He describes the
long drawn out suffering of the people (5–7). III. He reminds God
of what care he once had for Israel, his vine (9–12). IV. The vine is
now in a sad condition; it needs God's protection (13–16). V. Let

the enemy perish and Israel be restored, is the psalmist's prayer; in
the future, he says, the Israelites will be faithful (17–19). The
refrain, vv. 4, 8, 20, is repeated three times.

1 To the choirmaster. To the melody, "The Lily of the Law." A
   psalm of Asaph.

I   2 O you who shepherd Israel, give ear,
       you who are leading Joseph like a flock!
       Enthroned above the Cherubim, may your glance appear
    3 before Manasses, Ephraim, and Benjamin!
       Awake your might, and come to rescue us!
    4 O God, restore us:
       to save us, show your kindly face!

II 5 O God of hosts, how long will you resent,
       although your people prays?
    6 For food, you give to them the bread of tears;
       you give them copious tears for drink!
    7 A subject of dispute you made us 'mongst our neighbors;
       our foes laugh us to scorn!
    8 O God of hosts, restore us:
       to save us, show your kindly face!

III 9 You brought the vine from Egypt,
       you drove the heathens out, and planted it,
   10 for which you had prepared the soil;
       and it struck root and overspread the land;
   11 the hills were mantled with its shade,
       and with its shoots God's cedar trees.
   12 It stretched its runners down to the sea,
       its scions, to the stream.

IV 13 Then why have you destroyed its fence?
       All passers-by now pluck its fruit!
   14 The wild boar lays it waste;
       the roving beasts now graze on it!
   15 O God of hosts, return! Look down from heaven,
       and see, and to this vine a visit pay!

79:7. A subject of dispute: their neighbors disagreed about the division
of the booty which they had taken from the Israelites.

79:11b. God's cedar trees: these trees are so old, so tall, and so developed,
that it seems as though God himself might have planted them.

16 Protect the vine — your right hand planted it —
the sprig — you made it hale and strong for your own sake!

V 17 May those who cut it down and burnt it up
be ruined by your frown!

18 Your hand rest on the man your hand has raised,
the mortal whom you made so hale and strong for your own sake.

19 No more shall we be false to you;
keep us alive, and we will glorify your name.

20 *Lord, God of hosts, restore us!*
To save us, show your kindly face!

PSALM 80

A Hymn and a Warning on a Solemn Feast Day

This psalm was probably sung in the liturgy of a solemn feast (either
of the Pasch or that of the Tabernacles). It has two parts: the first
part (A) is a hymn in which the Israelites are invited to celebrate
the feast instituted by God (2–6b); the second (B) is an admoni-
tion; here God himself is the speaker (6c–17). I. He reminds the
Israelites of their deliverance from Egypt and of the legislation given
on Sinai; he reminds them also of the law which prescribed that
they should worship the one true God alone (7–11). II. He com-
plains that the people have not obeyed him; it is the obedient ones
who will have the protection of God from their enemies and a
generous blessing (12–17).

1 *To the choirmaster. To the melody, "The Wine Presses." A*
psalm of Asaph.

A 2 Exult in God our helper,
and Jacob's God acclaim!

3 Sound the harp, strike the tambourine,
the sweetly sounding cither and the lyre.

4 The trumpet blow: the moon is new,
the moon is full, on this our festive day.

79:18. *the man your hand has raised:* i.e., Israel (spoken of as a vine in
v. 16), whom the hand of God had planted. This line is a repetition of v.
16, with the metaphor dropped.

80:4. Special sacrifices were offered at the time of the new moon, during
which the sacred trumpets were blown. The feasts of the Pasch and the
Tabernacles were begun on the day of the full moon.

5 It is an old established rule for Israel,
   a precept made by Jacob's God.
6 For Joseph he has made this law,
   when, spite of Egypt, he went forth.

B   I heard a voice I did not know before:
I   7 "I freed his shoulder from the load;
        his hands dropped from the hod.
     8 In your distress you cried, and I delivered you;
        and from a thundering cloud I answered you,
        and at the waters of Meriba tested you.
     9 My people, list: I will admonish you.
        If you would only hear me, Israel!
    10 You shall not have a foreign god;
        and not adore an alien deity.
    11 I am the Lord, your God!
        From Egypt I have led you forth:
        then open wide your mouth, and I shall fill it full!

II 12 Alas, my people did not hear my voice,
        and Israel was not submissive to my will.
    13 Therefore I gave them over to their callousness;
        now let them shift according as they please!
    14 Would that my people heeded me;
        and would that Israel walked my ways!
    15 At once would I put down their foes,
        and turn my hand against their enemies.
    16 Then those who hate the Lord would flatter him:
        their doom would be forever sealed!
    17 But Israel — I would nourish it with most delicious wheat,
        and feed it full with honey from the rock."

80:6c. A priest or prophet seems to be introduced as speaking here.
80:11c. Cf. v. 17.
80:16. Even though unwillingly, they would yet subject themselves to him.
80:17b. *honey from the rock:* so great will be the abundance of honey
that it will flow from rocks and stones.

PSALM 81

The Final End of Unjust Judges

God is introduced as condemning unjust judges. I. He rebukes their injustice, which favors the wicked, and oppresses the humble (2–4). II. He is convinced that they are set in their ways; they disturb the whole order of things; he predicts for them an ignominious death (5–7). The psalmist asks God to pass judgment at once on these unworthy men (8).

1 A *psalm of Asaph.*

In the divine assembly rises God,
and in the midst of gods he acts as judge!

I   2 "How long will you unjustly judge
and champion the cause of impious men?
3 Defend the orphan, the oppressed;
see justice done to poor and lowly men!
4 Set free the needy, the oppressed;
and from the grip of rascals rescue them!"

II   5 They have no sense! They do not understand!
Wrapt in gloom, they grope about!
And all the pillars of our land are rocked!
6 Though I have stated: "You are gods,
and children, each and all, of the Most High,
7 yet, nonetheless, like mortals you shall die,
and fall like any human prince."
8 Rise, God, and judge the earth;
all nations are your rightful property!

81:1b. *in the midst of gods:* judges and magistrates are here called *gods* because they act in the place of God and judge and govern in his name and by his authority (cf. Ps. 57:2).

81:6, 7. God had given them authority and power that they might act in his name. They will be stripped of these and die a wretched death.

Psalm 82

Against Enemies Joined to Oppose the Israelites

The psalm deals with some conspiracy of neighboring tribes and the Assyrians against Israel. I. The psalmist points out how certain peoples have made common cause against Israel; he lists the names of these peoples (2–9). II. He then asks God to reduce these enemies to nothingness, as he once before had reducd enemy chieftains. He figuratively describes their ruin, which will prepare for the universal reign of God (10–19).

¹ A song. A psalm of Asaph.

I   ² Do not be silent, Lord!
Do not be silent, God; do not be still!

³ You see, your foes are in tumultuous rage,
and those who hate you raise their heads.

⁴ To harm your race they hatch out plots;
against your clients they conspire.

⁵ "Come," they say, "let us destroy their nationhood;
no more must Israel's name be mentioned."

⁶ In truth, with one accord they lay their plans;
they form a league in your despite:

⁷ the tents of Edom and the Ismaelites,
the Moabites and Agarenes,

⁸ Gebal, Ammon, and Amalek;
Philistia and the Tyrians.

⁹ Assyria, too, makes common cause with them,
and lends its arms to the sons of Lot.

II   ¹⁰ Do to them what you did to Madian,
to Sisara, to Jabin by the Cison brook —

¹¹ the men that were at Endor killed,
that rotted on the ground like dung.

82:7–9. With the exception of the Assyrians, the tribes mentioned here were all neighbors of the Israelites. The pact referred to in v. 6 may not have been historical; the poet may have thus summed up the opposition of all peoples to the people of God.

82:9b. *the sons of Lot*: the Moabites and Ammonites, who seem to have been the leaders in this league against the Israelites.

12 Deal with their chieftains as with Zeb and Oreb,
   with all their leaders as with Zebee and Salmana,
13 whose boast had been:
   "Let us invade the regions set apart for God."
14 My God, make them like leaves caught in a whirl of wind.
   like stubble swept off by a gust.
15 As fire that burns a forest down,
   and as a flame that sears the mountainsides —
16 so may your tempest drive them off;
   so may your storm put them to rout.
17 O may their face be mantled with disgrace,
   that they may look up to your name, O Lord;
18 or else, be shame and terror their eternal lot;
   be they confounded and destroyed!
19 For they must know that you alone, whose name is "Lord,"
   are throned on high o'er all the earth.

PSALM 83

The Psalmist's Longing for the Temple

I. The psalmist desires to go to the temple of God (2–4). II. Blessed
are they, he says, who can delay there always and those also who
are starting their pilgrimage to the temple (5–8). III. He begs God's
blessing and sings of the happiness of those who linger in the courts
of the Lord (9–13).

1 To the choirmaster. To the melody, "The Wine Presses." Of the
  sons of Core. A psalm.

I 2 How lovely is your dwelling place, O Lord of hosts!
   3 My spirit pines — for the courts of the Lord it faints with yearning.
     My body and my soul
     exult in longing for the living God.
   4 The sparrow even finds a home,
     the swallow for herself, a nest wherein to lodge her young:
     your altars, Lord of hosts,
     my King, my God!

II 5 O well for those who dwell within your house, O Lord,
unceasing is their praise of you.
6 Blest is the man who draws from you his strength,
while on a holy pilgrimage his mind is bent.
7 Cross such as he an arid vale, they change it to a place of springs,
and early rain will clothe it with its blessings.
8 They wend their way and grow in strength;
in Sion they will see the God of gods!

III 9 O hear my prayer, O Lord of hosts!
O hearken, Jacob's God!
10 Look, God, our shield!
Look at the brow of your anointed one!
11 In truth, one day spent in your courts
is better than a thousand others.
I fain would hug the threshold of the house of my God
rather than dwell in sinners' tents.
12 A sun and a shield is the Lord God:
both grace and glory the Lord vouchsafes.
No blessings he denies to those
who walk the ways of innocence!
13 O Lord of hosts,
how happy is the man who trusts in you!

PSALM 84

"His Redemption Is at Hand"

The psalmist depicts the conditions of the exiles, who, after the decree of Cyrus (538 B.C.) were returning to Judea.

I. As they are returning, they are beset with difficulties, but God, they know, has forgiven the sins of his people and has set aside his wrath (2–4). II. The exiles ask him to complete the work of saving them, and to give them once again a happy life (5–8). III. Finally,

---

83:7. The pilgrims, moved by holy expectation and faith, look upon arid stretches as though they were valleys abounding in springs and lush verdure.

83:8. As they make their way, they feel themselves growing stronger; they have one thing in mind, that is, that they will see God.

83:10b. After they have arrived at the temple, they pray for the *anointed* one, i.e., the king.

a prophet or priest, hearing within himself the voice of God, announces that salvation is close at hand, and that the Lord will come surrounded, as it were, by a retinue of justice, mercy, peace, and prosperity (9–14).

The psalm refers to the messianic salvation that is to come from God.

1 *To the choirmaster. A psalm of the sons of Core.*

I   2 To your land, O Lord, you have been kind,
and given a happy turn to Jacob's lot.
3 You have dismissed your people's guilt,
and all their sins removed from sight.
4 You have repressed your angry mood,
and ceased the fury of your wrath.

II   5 Reinstate us, our savior, God,
and lay aside the indignation you have felt for us.
6 Will you be wroth with us forevermore?
will you extend your wrath from age to age?
7 O will you not restore our life?
Shall not your people find their joy in you?
8 Show us your mercy, Lord,
and your redemption grant to us!

III   9 Now will I listen to the Lord God's words;
assuredly, his words are words of peace,
meant for his people and his saints,
for all that turn to him wholeheartedly.
10 For, surely, his redemption is at hand for those who worship him;
and in our land shall glory make its home.
11 Then mercy and fidelity will amicably meet;
justice and peace will kiss each other.
12 Fidelity will sprout upon the earth;
justice will glance from heaven above.
13 Also, the Lord will grant prosperity;
our land will yield its fruit.

84:9. The prophet, feeling that he is divinely illuminated, waits for God to speak.

84:11, 12. The mercy of God and the fidelity of the people, the justice of God and the peace of men, the fidelity of men and the justice of God will come together; heaven and earth will unite in peace and love. And earthly blessings will not be lacking (cf. v. 13).

14 Justice will herald his advance,
salvation wait upon his every step.

PSALM 85

Prayer of a Good Servant of God When in Trouble

The psalm opens (I, 1–7) and closes (III, 11–17) with a prayer;
between these there is a short hymn honoring the omnipotence of
God (II, 8–10).
    I. Reasons are urged why God should give his help: his goodness
and mercy (5), the wretchedness of the servant making the petition
(1, 7), the servant's devotion and faithfulness (2), his persevering
prayer (3, 4, 6). II. A hymn of praise (8–10). III. Next are indicated
the favors asked for: the grace of leading a good life (11) and aid
against enemies (14–17).

1 A prayer of David.

I   Incline your ear, Lord; answer me:
      poor and forlorn am I!
2 Protect me, for to you I am devoted!
      Save your servant trusting you!
      My God are you!
3 Have mercy on me, Lord;
      incessantly I cry to you.
4 Make glad your servant's soul, O Lord,
      because to you I lift my soul.
5 Aye, you, O Lord, are good and kind
      and full of mercy toward your worshipers.
6 Then hear, O Lord, my prayer,
      and listen to my pleading voice.
7 In this my evil hour I cry to you:
      I know that you will answer me.

II **8** You have no peer among the gods, O Lord;
      there is no work like unto yours.
    9 For, all the nations you have made

84:14. Justice and *salvation*, as in a retinue, will accompany God, the
Saviour.
    85:8. *among the gods:* i.e., among the spirits (angels) who hover about
God (cf. Ps. 88:7, 8), or, and perhaps more correctly, among those who are
called gods (cf. vv. 8, 10).

will come and pay you homage, Lord,
and hymn the praises of your name.
10 Yes, great you are, and you do wondrous things!
Yes, you alone are God.

III 11 Teach me your way, O Lord: your truth shall guide my steps;
direct my heart, that it may reverence your name.
12 With all my heart I wish to hymn your praise, O Lord, my God,
and glorify your name eternally.
13 Your mercy toward me has been great:
you snatched me from the deep abyss.
14 O God, proud men arose to do me harm;
a horde of tyrants plots against my life;
to you they pay no heed.
15 But you, O Lord, are a kind and merciful God,
to anger slow, beyond all bounds merciful and mild.
16 O look on me and pity me;
lend to your servant your own strength,
and save your handmaid's son.
17 A token of your favor grant to me:
my foes shall be ashamed when they perceive
that you have comforted and helped me, Lord.

PSALM 86

Sion, the Fatherland of All Peoples

The psalm is a prophetic vision of the messianic Sion which will be the fatherland of all peoples and the fount of all good things.

God loves this Sion, and glorious things are said of it (1–3). In it are said to be born all men and every nation (4–6), and to it are ascribed all the good things which they enjoy (7).

1 *A psalm of the sons of Core. A song.*

His own foundation on the holy hills,

85:17. The psalmist asks God to confirm, by some sign, the aid that he has given him.

86:1b. *His own foundation: foundation* (the abstract is here used for the concrete) means that which God founded, i.e., by a parallelism, Sion. The prophet, almost ravished by the beauty and glory of the citadel of God, breaks forth into its praises.

² the Lord loves it —
the gates of Sion — more than all of Jacob's tents!
³ What glorious things are said of you,
O citadel of God!
⁴ "Rahab as well as Babel will I count among my worshipers;
aye, and Philistia, too, and Tyre, and the Ethiopian race —
here these were born!
⁵ Of Sion Mount it shall be said: 'All, man for man, were born in it;
himself, the Most High, 'stablished it!' "
⁶ The Lord will in the book of nations write:
"Here these were born!"
⁷ And they shall sing in festal dance:
"My fountains all — they are in you!"

Psalm 87

Prayer of a Man Seriously Ill

The psalmist, afflicted with a revolting disease (it may have been leprosy; cf. v. 9) has only God to console him.
I. He describes the gravity of his condition, which will cause his death, and which has already separated him from friends and relatives (2–9). II. He asks God to help him, while he is yet alive, for, certainly, it is the living and not the dead who can praise God (10–13). III. He tells of his loneliness and desolation (14–19).

¹ A song. A psalm of the sons of Core. To the choirmaster. To the melody, "Mahalat." For singing. A maskil of Heman the Ezrahite.

I ² O Lord, my God, I cry to you by day;
by night I wail before your throne.
³ O may my pleading make its way to you;
and to my cry incline your ear!

86:4. Rahab: i.e., Egypt and Babel, the two great idolatrous kingdoms, will be counted among the worshipers of God and will be the sons of Sion; in fact, all peoples (v. 5), man for man, will be looked upon as born in Sion.
86:7. The peoples in exultation will proclaim that all good things come to them from Sion.

⁴ Alas, my soul is cloyed with grief;
my life is on the brink of death.
⁵ I count as one of those who sink into the pit;
like to a weak, decrepit man I am!
⁶ Among the dead my couch is ready-made;
as good as slain I am, as one laid in the sepulchre:
no more do you remember them,
and from your loving care they are cut off.
⁷ For you have bedded me deep in the pit,
in darkness, in a whirling pool.
⁸ Your indignation heavily weighs on me;
with all your floods you are engulfing me.
⁹ My friends — you keep them far away from me:
you made them loathe me utterly;
shut in I am, and there is no escape for me.

II ¹⁰ My eyes grow dim from wretchedness:
I cry to you, Lord, every day;
to you I stretch my hands.
¹¹ Do you work wonders for the dead?
Or will the dead arise and give you praise?
¹² And is your goodness talked of in the sepulchre,
your faithfulness a theme among the dead?
¹³ And are your wonders mentioned in the gloom;
your kindness, where oblivion reigns?

III ¹⁴ But I — I cry to you, O Lord;
at dawn my prayer goes up to you.
¹⁵ Why, Lord, do you repel my soul,
why hide your face from me?
¹⁶ I am a wretch, from childhood doomed to die;
your terrors I have borne and — pine away!
¹⁷ O'er me your angry bursts have passed;
your terrors shatter me;
¹⁸ like water they surround me constantly;
they all at once encircle me.
¹⁹ Friend and comrade you have kept away from me;
dark and gloom are my companions.

87:11, 12. Cf. Pss. 6:6; 29:10; 113B:17; Isa. 38:18 f.
87:13b. *where oblivion reigns:* where man now knows nothing of the earth.

Psalm 88

Ruin of the House of David Compared With the Promises God Once Made to David

This psalm was probably composed at the beginning of the exile; in it the author considers the sad lot of the royal house of David, and this he compares with the splendid promises once made to David by the Lord.

I. The psalmist recalls the promises of God (2–5). II. His faith and hope are strengthened at the thought of God's greatness and power (6–19). With this God no other can be compared (6–9); he is the all-powerful Creator, and the just governor of the world (10–15); the protector and king of his people (16–19). III. The promises once given to David and his house are enumerated (20–38): God chose David and will sustain him (20–22); he will defend him against his enemies and extend his kingdom (23–26); he will make him greater than other kings and establish his throne forever (27–30); even though David's descendants should sin, he will not withdraw his favor from the house of David (31–34); this pact, entered into with David, will never be set aside (35–38). IV. With these splendid promises, the psalmist compares the present sorrowful state of affairs (39–42); the enemies have triumphed and David's throne is overthrown (43–46). V. Overwhelmed by such calamities, he beseeches God that he will not be unmindful of his ancient promises, and that he will help his anointed one and take from him the disgrace that has come upon him (47–52). Verse 53 is a doxology with which Book 3 of the Psalms closes.

1 A maskil of Ethan the Ezrahite.

I 2 The mercies of the Lord I will forever chant,
from age to age declare his faithfulness.
3 For you have said: "Grace is assured forevermore,"
and in the firmament you guarantee your faithfulness.
4 "I made a covenant with my elect,
and to my servant David I have sworn:
5 'Your line will I make permanent,
and will secure your throne from age to age.' "

II 6 The heavens hymn your wondrous deeds, O Lord;
the court of saints, your faithfulness!

88:6b. *the court of saints:* i.e., of the angels, who, in v. 7, are referred to as *the sons of God.*

7 Above the clouds — who can compare with the Lord?
Who can be like the Lord among the sons of God?
8 Dreadful in the council of the saints is God,
great and awful above all those around him.
9 Lord, God of hosts, who is your peer?
Mighty you are, O Lord, and girt with faithfulness.

10 The prideful sea you command;
the tumult of the waves you curb.
11 You pierced and set your foot on Rahab;
your mighty arm dispersed your foes.
12 Yours are the heavens, yours the earth;
the globe and all that fills it you secured;
13 the northwind you created and the south;
Thabor's and Hermon's pride is in your name.
14 You wield a mighty arm;
firm and high-uplifted is your hand.
15 Right and justice pave your throne;
grace and fidelity herald your advance.

16 Well for the people skilled in holding jubilee:
they bask, Lord, in your beaming smile.
17 Your name is their unbroken happiness;
your justice is their pride.
18 You are the splendor of their might,
your favor is the wellspring of our strength.
19 Our shield is in the hands of the Lord,
our king, the ward of Israel's Holy One.

III 20 In a vision of yore you addressed your saints
and said: "I crowned a mighty man,
and from the people raised my chosen one.

88:11. *Rahab,* a monster personifying pride and rebellion. Some hold that Rahab stands for Egypt (cf. Ps. 86:4). The waters mentioned in v. 10 are those which covered the earth at creation. Here they are looked upon as enemies with whom God fights (cf. Ps. 73:13).

88:15b. *grace . . . fidelity:* these are said to be members of God's retinue.

88:19. *Our shield:* that is, our protector, the king, enjoys God's care; he is *the ward of Israel's Holy One,* that is, God. This verse forms a transition to the following section.

88:20. *your saints:* God spoke to the prophet Nathan (see 2 Sam. 7:8–16) and through him to King David and the chosen people.

21 I found my servant David,
and with my holy oil anointed him.
22 My hand shall always be with him;
my arm shall strengthen him.

23 No foe shall catch him in a snare,
no enemy shall get the best of him.
24 No, I will crush all those confronting him,
and all who hate him put to rout.
25 My grace and my fidelity shall be his bodyguard;
his might shall be exalted in my name.
26 O'er the sea will I extend his sway,
his arm to where the rivers flow.

27 To me he will call out: 'My sire are you,
my God, the bedrock of my weal.'
28 I will appoint him as my first-born Son,
supreme among earth's kings.
29 Forever will I keep him in my grace;
my covenant with him shall firmly stand.
30 His line will I make permanent,
his throne — as long as heaven lasts.

31 Should e'er his line forsake my law,
and never in my precepts have their rule of life;
32 if ever they infringe the statutes I enact,
and do not cherish my decrees:
33 then will I visit with the rod their guilt,
and punish their misdeeds with stripes.
34 Yet will I not withdraw my grace from him,
and not belie my plighted word.

35 I will not violate my covenant,
nor change what I have solemnly declared.
36 I once for all swore by my holiness;
to David, surely, I shall not be false.
37 His line is to endure eternally;
as the sun, his throne shall ever last before me,

88:26. *the sea:* the Mediterranean; *the rivers* are the Euphrates and its tributaries. The prophecy refers to the universal reign of the Messias, the son of David.

38 and as the moon, which lasts eternally
   a faithful witness in the firmament."

IV 39 But now — your rejection is complete and absolute!
   Grievously wroth are you with your anointed one!
40 You spurned your servant's covenant,
   and in the dust defiled his crown.
41 You crushed the bulwarks all around him,
   and laid in ruins all his battlements.
42 All passers-by have plundered him;
   a laughingstock is he to neighboring tribes.

43 His enemies' might you have reared high,
   and filled with rapture all his foes.
44 His sword's edge you blunted,
   and did not prop him in the fray.
45 You made his splendor ebb away,
   and hurled his throne down on the ground.
46 The days of his prime you shortened,
   and wrapped him round with shame.

V 47 How long, O Lord? Will you hide yourself forever?
   And shall your indignation flame like fire?
48 Recall how brief my life is,
   how frail you have created man!
49 Where is the man who lives and never shall taste death?
   Who from death's grasp can wrest his life?
50 Where are your ancient mercies, Lord,
   which you have pledged to David by your faithfulness?
51 Remember, Lord, your servants' shame:
   the hate of all the heathen tribes comes home to me,
52 wherewith your adversaries, Lord —
   wherewith, at every step, they taunt your own anointed one!

53 The Lord be blest eternally!
   So let it be! so let it be!

88:39–46. The psalmist is here speaking, not only of the affliction of
David and his house, but also of that of the whole people; the ruin of the
people is also the ruin of the king.
88:48, 49. The psalmist hopes to see the end of so many and such great
evils before he dies.

BOOK 4: Psalms 89-105

PSALM 89

Man's Life Is Brief;
Let the Eternal God Be His Refuge Always

I. The psalmist compares God, the eternal and omnipotent One, the refuge of all generations, with man, who lives but a short span (1–6). II. The lot of man is sorrowful and hard because, by his sins, he has provoked the wrath of God (7–11). III. He asks God to bring men back to their senses and to reward them for the sufferings of life. He prays that, ultimately, God's glory may appear (12–17).

1 A prayer of Moses, the man of God.

I   O Lord, a haven you have been to us
from age to age!
2 Ere mountains came to be,
ere earth and world were born —
from all eternity, you are eternal, God.
3 To dust you bid all mortals to return;
you say: "Children of men, return!"
4 A thousand years are in your sight
no more than yesterday, already past —
and like a nightly watch!
5 You snatch men off — like a morning dream they are!
How like the freshly sprouting grass they are!
6 At morn it greens and blooms;
at even it is cut and fades!

II 7 In truth, we are the victims of your wrath,
and by your indignation we are terrified.

89:2. The origin of the earth is no more to the eternal God than the birth of a human being.

89:3. One word of God suffices to bring to an end a human life.

89:4c. The night watch was a third part of the night. Hence here the terms means a very brief period.

89:5, 6. The grass, springing up in the morning, withers rapidly under the hot oriental sun (cf. Pss. 102:15 ff.; 128:6; Isa. 40:6 ff.).

89:7. The span of man's life is very brief. This brevity terrifies him, but he cannot escape it. It is a punishment of sin (cf. Gen. 3:17–20).

⁸ You keep our guilt in constant view,
our hidden sins before your searching eye.
⁹ For, all our days rolled by o'ershadowed by your ire;
we spent our years just as we heave a sigh!
¹⁰ Our life's whole span is seventy years,
or eighty, if we are robust;
and most of them are idle toil!
they quickly pass and — we take wing!
¹¹ O who can weigh the fierceness of your ire,
who gage your wrath, as the fear due you deserves!

III ¹² Teach us to number o'er our days,
so that we may attain to wisdom of the heart.
¹³ Return, O Lord — how long?
Be gracious to your loyal ones;
¹⁴ and with your mercy sate us speedily,
that we may spend in raptures all our days.
¹⁵ O give us joy to compensate the days when you afflicted us,
the years in which we tasted misery.
¹⁶ Let on your servants dawn your masterwork,
your glory, on their sons.
¹⁷ The goodness of the Lord our God descend on us;
and speed the work of our own hands for us.
O speed the work of our poor hands!

PSALM 90

The All-High God, Protector of the Just

I. The psalmist, in various figures, shows that he who trusts in the Lord is protected by him and watched over by his angels (1–13). II. In this second part, God himself speaks; he assures the psalmist that he will hear his prayers (14–16).

I ¹ You dwell beneath the shelter of the Most High?
You rest beneath the shade of the Omnipotent?
² Then say to the Lord: "My haven and my citadel,
my God, in whom I trust!"

89:11. The verse means: who understands the fierceness of God's anger against sin, and who fears him with that reverential awe that would prevent sin?

3 'Tis he will save you from the fowler's snare,
from every baneful thing.
4 His wings will shelter you;
his pinions are your safe retreat.
A shield and buckler is his faithfulness.
5 No fear for you of nightly terror,
of arrows shot by day,
6 of mischief stalking in the dark,
of havoc rampant in the noonday light.
7 A thousand fall upon your left and tens of thousands on your right:
no harm comes near to you.
8 But you will look about with your own eyes,
and see the sinners' punishment.
9 Your refuge is the Lord;
you made the Most High God your bulwark.
10 No ill shall, therefore, come to you;
no scourge approach your tent.
11 He gave his angels charge of you
to keep you safe in all your ways:
12 upon their hands they bear you up,
lest you should dash your foot against a stone.
13 On asp and viper you will tread,
and lion and serpent trample down.

II 14 "Because he clings to me, I will deliver him,
and shield him; for he knows my name.
15 He will appeal to me, and I will hear his prayer;
in tribulation, I shall be with him.
16 An ample length of days I will bestow on him;
my blessings I will grant to him."

90:5. *nightly terror:* this might mean a thief, or, more probably, an enemy attacking by night.

90:5b. *arrows shot by day:* probably stands for an open attack by the enemy.

90:6. *mischief stalking in the dark:* means an epidemic disease; night air was thought to be favorable for the spread of sickness.

90:6b. *havoc rampant in the noonday light:* this probably refers to the fierce heat of the noonday sun, or, again, it may refer to the simoon, a deadly wind which was prevalent in southern deserts. It was particularly harmful around midday.

Psalm 91

Praise of God
as Wisely and Justly Governing Human Affairs

I. The psalmist calls on all men to honor God's goodness and faith-fulness (2–5). II. The ruin that comes to sinners is evidence that God, in all wisdom, governs the fate of men (6–9). III. The triumph that good men enjoy reveals this same thing (10–12). IV. The poet lauds God's goodness to righteous men (13–16).

¹ A psalm. A song. For the Sabbath day.

I ² 'Tis good to celebrate the Lord,
make melody in honor of your name, Most High:
³ to blaze your mercy at the break of dawn;
your faithfulness, by night,
⁴ with lyre and ten-stringed psaltery,
with song to harp's accompaniment.
⁵ For by your deeds, O Lord, you gladden me;
your handiwork is my delight.

II ⁶ O how magnificent are all your works, O Lord;
and how profound your thoughts!
⁷ The senseless do not know these things,
the foolish do not understand.
⁸ Let sinners thrive like luscious grass,
let evil men bask in prosperity:
yet are they to eternal ruin doomed!
⁹ But you, O Lord, for all eternity you are supreme.

III ¹⁰ Indeed, O Lord, indeed, your foes —
indeed, your foes are doomed;
aye, evil men shall vanish, each and all!
¹¹ You gave me strength as of a buffalo;
and on me poured out oil most pure.
¹² And now my eye looks down upon my enemies;
my ears hear happy news about my vicious foes.

91:11. The *buffalo* is taken as a symbol of strong and indomitable courage; *pure oil*, as that of riches and wealth.

IV ¹³ A holy man thrives like a palm,
grows like a cedar on Mount Lebanon.
¹⁴ And, planted in the house of the Lord,
such men shall flourish in the courts of God.
¹⁵ In ripe old age, they still bear fruit,
and hale and hearty they are like a fresh green plant.
¹⁶ Thus they proclaim how right remains the Lord,
my rock! In him there is no wrong!

PSALM 92

The Lord Is Powerful King of the World

This hymn honors God as the Lord of creation. The poet sees God
as king, clothed in majesty and power, seated on his throne, which
is from all eternity (1, 2). He contemplates the roaring surges of
rivers and seas; God, he says, is mightier than these (3, 4). He concludes that God's word is worthy of complete allegiance; his earthly
habitation, the Temple, should be shown the greatest reverence (5).

¹ The Lord is king, and robed in majesty!
The Lord is robed and girt with might!
'Tis he has made the world secure:
and it shall stand unmoved!
² Firm is your throne from ancient days;
aye, from eternity you are!
³ The rivers surge, O Lord,
the rivers surge their voice;
the rivers surge their thundering roar!
⁴ Mightier far than heaving waves,
mightier far than seething sea,
aye, mighty is the Lord on high!
⁵ Most worthy are your promises of faith;
and holiness, O Lord, your house beseems for endless length
of days!

91:14. *planted*: i.e., good men (cf. v. 13) who, remaining close to the
Lord, like trees planted in the courts of the Temple, receive special graces
from him, which help them even unto old age.
92:5. *promises*: i.e., the Revelation which God gave through the prophets.

PSALM 93
God Is Invoked for Help Against Wicked Oppressors

The poet in this psalm expresses anger at the conduct of proud, godless oppressors of his people. A. In the first part (1–11) he calls down the vengeance of God upon them. I. Evildoers do not desist (1–4). II. He points out their crimes and blasphemies (5–7). III. He rebukes the foolishness and perversity of these men; they can hide nothing from God (8–11). B. In the second part (12–23) the psalmist states that he had always put his trust in God. I. God will not desert his people, but will see to it that justice prevails (12–15). II. God's grace and consolation sustain the psalmist (16–19). III. Hence, whatever may be the designs of wicked men, he knows that God will protect him and destroy them (20–23).

A I   1 Avenger God, O Lord!
          Avenger God, O let your glance appear!
     2 Arise, you who judge the earth!
          Give to the proud what they deserve!
     3 How long, O Lord, shall godless men,
          how long shall godless men exult?
     4 How long shall evildoers boast and brag,
          and vaunt their insolence?

  II   5 Your people, Lord, they trample down;
          your heritage they plague.
     6 Both guest and widow they dispatch,
          and slay the fatherless.
     7 And then they say: "The Lord — he does not see!
          The God of Jacob does not mind!"

  III   8 Come to your senses, foolish folk!
          When will you, fools, be wise?
     9 Will he who made the ear not hear?
          Will he who formed the eye not see?
    10 He, the nations' Teacher, will he not chastise —
          he who teaches men the lore they have?
    11 The Lord can read men's thoughts;
          he knows that they are void of sense.

93:7. Cf. Ps. 9B:4, 11, 13.

B I ¹² Well for the man whom you instruct, O Lord,
and train to read your law,
¹³ that you may comfort him in evil days
until the pit is dug for godless men.
¹⁴ No, no; the Lord will not reject his race
or cast away his heritage!
¹⁵ Some day just retribution shall be made,
and all true hearts will welcome it!

II ¹⁶ Who will rise in my defense against my foes,
who by me stand and smite the wicked horde?
¹⁷ But for the Lord, my help,
I soon should in the house of silence dwell!
¹⁸ And when I think: "My foot is slipping!"
your grace, O Lord, is my support.
¹⁹ When worries throng my heart,
your consolations are my soul's delight.

III ²⁰ Could e'er injustice touch your judgment seat,
cause mischief under pretext of the law?
²¹ Let them assail a holy man,
and guiltless blood condemn.
²² The Lord will surely be my guard;
my God will be my safe retreat.
²³ He will repay them for their evil deeds,
and their own wickedness will ruin them.
Indeed, the Lord our God will ruin them!

PSALM 94

A Call to Praise God and Render Him Obedience

The psalmist cites two reasons why the Israelites should praise God.
I. He is the king of the whole world; he it is who created it (3–5).
II. He is the shepherd of his people Israel (7). All owe obedience
to him lest they be cast aside as their fathers once were in the
desert (8–11). Twice the psalmist issues a call to praise God
(1–2, 6).

93:17b. *in the house of silence:* i.e., in the place of the dead.

I ¹ O come; let us exult in the Lord!
Let us acclaim the rock, our savior!
 ² With praises let us go to meet his face;
let us exult in God with songs!
 ³ Indeed, the Lord — he is a mighty God,
a mighty king above all gods!
 ⁴ Earth's depths are in his palm;
the mountain peaks are his.
 ⁵ His is the sea: he has created it;
his is the land: his hands have fashioned it.

II ⁶ Come, then; let us fall down; let us adore
and bend the knee before the Lord who has created us.
 ⁷ For he — he is our God!
We are the people of his pasturing, the sheep led by his hand.

Would that today you listened to his voice:
 ⁸ "O harden not your hearts as in Meriba you once did,
as on the day of Massa in the wilderness,
 ⁹ 'twas there your fathers tempted me;
they tested me though they had seen my works.
¹⁰ For forty years I loathed this brood of men;
'Wayward of heart this people is!' I said,
'They do not know my ways.'
¹¹ I therefore in my anger swore:
'Into my place of rest they shall not come!' "

Psalm 95

Praise God, King of All the Earth

The psalmist envisions the coming of the Lord, at the end of time, to establish the messianic kingdom (13). I. He exhorts all to praise this great king (1–3). II. He alone is God, full of majesty, power, and splendor (4–6). III. To him, let all people give praise, offer sacrifices, render homage; for now he begins to reign (7–10). IV. Let nature itself rejoice because God comes to rule the earth (11–13).

94:8. God is introduced as speaking here. At Meriba and Massa, the Israelites had murmured against God.

I   1   Sing to the Lord a song not sung before!
     O universal earth, sing to the Lord!
  2   Sing to the Lord and bless his name;
     make his salvation known from day to day!
  3   Among the Gentiles voice his glory,
     in all the tribes, his wondrous deeds.

II   4   The Lord is great, deserving of the highest praise;
     let him be feared above all gods.
  5   Mere figments are the Gentile gods;
     it is the Lord who made the firmament.
  6   State and beauty herald his advance;
     might and splendor deck his holy shrine.

I   7   Acclaim the Lord, O tribes on tribes,
     acclaim the might and glory of the Lord.
  8   Acclaim the glorious name of the Lord.
     Enter his courts and offer sacrifice;
  9   in sacred vesture robed, adore the Lord.
     Before him tremble, universal earth!
  10   Among the Gentiles say: "The Lord is King!"
     Firm he made the globe so that it never should be moved;
     he rules the tribes with equity.

J   11   Rejoice, O firmament! Exult, O earth!
     O sea and all that fills you, roar applause!
  12   O fields and all that bide in you, be thrilled with joy!
     All forest trees shall now rejoice
  13   before the Lord: because he comes,
     he comes to rule the earth.
     Aye, he will rule the world with judgment just;
     all tribes, with judgment true.

PSALM 96

The Lord Confounds the Worshipers of False Gods; the True of Heart He Praises

This psalm, as the preceding one, deals with the coming of the Kingdom of God. I. God, manifesting himself through the phenomena of nature, appears for judgment (1–6). II. He puts to confusion the worshipers of idols; to just men he gives assurance of safety from enemies, and promises them light and joy (7–12).

I　1　The Lord is King! O earth, hold jubilee!
　　　Rejoice, O far-flung isles and coasts.
　　2　Clouds and gloom encircle him;
　　　right and justice pave his throne!
　　3　Fire heralds his advance,
　　　and it consumes his foes on every side.
　　4　His lightnings flash upon the world;
　　　the earth looks up and quakes!
　　5　Like wax, the mountains melt before the Lord,
　　　before the master of the universal earth.
　　6　The firmament proclaims his justice;
　　　his glory witness all the tribes!

II　7　All worshipers of graven gods are put to shame,
　　　and all who of their idols boast.
　　　Him all the gods adore on bended knee.
　　8　Mount Sion listens and exults,
　　　and Juda's citizens are jubilant,
　　　because your judgment, Lord, is near.
　　9　For over all the earth, O Lord, you are supreme,
　　　high-towering above all gods.
　　10　The Lord loves those who hate the wrong;
　　　he guards his dear devoted friends;
　　　from godless hands he rescues them.
　　11　Now light dawns on the innocent,
　　　and gladness on the true of heart.
　　12　Rejoice in the Lord, O holy souls,
　　　and celebrate his holy name.

96:2–6. There is a similar description of an appearance of God in Ps. 17:8–16.
96:7c. *gods:* i.e., those who were called gods by their worshipers.

PSALM 97

The Lord Is Victor, King, and Just Judge

I. The psalmist refers to a brilliant victory which God, without any
human help, has brought about for his people (1–3). II. He exhorts
all the people to rejoice (4–6). III. He bids nature itself to exult
over the power of God, the just judge, who comes to rule the earth
(7–9). This psalm is similar to Psalm 95. In both psalms, the subject
is messianic.

¹ A *psalm*.

I   Sing to the Lord a song not sung before:
       he has done wondrous things!
       His right hand brought his people victory;
       his holy arm accomplished it!
² The Lord made known his power to save;
       his justice he revealed for all the tribes to see.
³ He called to mind his goodness and fidelity
       and showed his grace to Israel's house.
       No corner of the earth but saw
       how well our God can save!

II   ⁴ Joy in the Lord, O universal earth!
       Rejoice! Hold jubilee with festal psalms!
⁵ Make music to the Lord upon the harp,
       with harp and sound of psaltery.
⁶ With trumpets and the blaring horn
       exult in sight of the Lord, our King.

I   ⁷ O sea and all that fills you, chant —
       O globe and all that dwell on you!
⁸ O rivers, clap your hands,
       joined by the mountains, which rejoice
⁹ to see the Lord, because he comes,
       he comes to rule the earth.
       He will rule the world with judgment just,
       all tribes, with judgment fair.

Psalm 98

The Holiness of the King

The general topic of this psalm is the kingdom of God. It puts special stress, however, on the holiness of God, which is made manifest in his kingdom. This holiness is emphasized in the refrains in vv. 3, 5, 9, which divide the psalm into three strophes. I. The Lord, present in the Temple, presiding over the Cherubim, asserts his rule over all people (1–3). II. Proper to his reign is justice, which he exercises in favor of the Israelites (4). III. Kindliness, too, is a quality of his reign, that kindliness with which he dealt with Moses, Aaron, and Samuel. When they were disobedient, he punished them, but never was he lacking in graciousness toward them (6–8). In the refrains, in vv. 5 and 9, the people are told to prostrate themselves before God, who is present above the Ark.

I   1 The Lord is King: the nations quake,
he thrones above the Cherubim: the earth is rocked.
  2 The Lord of Sion — he is great,
supreme above the nations, one and all.
  3 *O bid them praise your great and fearsome name;*
for it befits the Holy One.

II   4 He rules with might who justice loves.
You have established what is right.
Justice and right in Jacob you dispense.
  5 *Extol the Lord our God;*
before His footstool sink upon your knees:
for it befits the Holy One.

III   6 Moses and Aaron are among his priests;
and Samuel too called on his name;
they called upon the Lord: he answered them.
  7 Through pillar of cloud he spoke to them;
they heard all his decrees,
the precept which he gave to them.

98:1. On the top of the Ark were the images of two Cherubim. God's presence hovered above these figures. Hence he is said to throne there.
98:5b. The Ark is called the footstool of the Lord (cf. 1 Par. 28:2; Ps. 131:7).

⁸ O Lord, our God, you answered them;
and gracious, God, you were to them;
and yet you punished every fault of theirs.
⁹ *Extol the Lord our God;*
before his holy mountain sink upon your knees:
for holy is the Lord our God.

Psalm 99

Hymn Sung When Entering the Temple

This psalm was probably sung during the solemn entry of the people
into the Temple (2, 4). Not only are the Israelites invited to enter
the Temple, but all dwellers on the earth are bid to come, for God
is the creator and shepherd of all (2, 3). God is good and merciful
(5).

¹ *A psalm. For thanksgiving.*

Rejoice in the Lord, O universal earth!
² With gladness serve the Lord.
Appear before his eyes
with hearts all jubilant.
³ Know that the Lord is God:
'tis he that made us; his we are,
his people and the sheep of his own pasturing.
⁴ Enter his gates with praise upon your lips;
his courts, with hymns of praise.
Give thanks to him and bless his name.
⁵ The Lord is good, indeed;
his mercy lasts forevermore;
from age to age lasts his fidelity!

98:8c. Moses and Aaron were the ones whose faults were punished (cf.
Num. 20).
99:3c. Cf. Pss. 22:1; 94:7; Jn. 10:1–16.

Psalm 100

Resolutions of a Model Ruler

Here the psalmist depicts a model ruler, one who has as the basic principles of his government kindliness and justice. Such a man gives due praise to God (1), he so cultivates integrity of life that he is worthy of the divine presence (2), he puts away from himself all injustice and spurns all wicked men, detractors, and the proud of heart (3–5); but the just, the faithful, reliable men he uses in his administration (6); on sinners, he passes severe judgment; the city he rids of all evildoers (7, 8).

1 A psalm of David.

Let grace and justice be my theme;
to you, O Lord, I sing a song.
2 My way of life shall be unstained:
when will you come to visit me?
I give full scope to my high intent
amidst my homely scenes.
3 The goal I set before my eyes
shall be no evil thing.
I hate all men that take a crooked course:
not one of them shall be my confidant.
4 Let not the false of heart come near to me;
I will not cherish what is base.
5 The secret slanderer of his fellow man
I will destroy;
the haughty eye, the puffed-up heart
I will not brook.
6 My eye will search the land for honest souls,
that they may dwell with me;
and only men above reproach
shall be my servants.
7 Not welcome to my home
shall be a guileful man.
The one that falsifies
shall stand not in my presence.

8 Day after day I will destroy
the evildoers of the land,
and I will purge the city of the Lord
of men determined to do wrong.

PSALM 101

Lament and Prayers of One in Anguish

This psalm, which is the fifth of the penitential psalms, has three parts. I. A certain man, afflicted and sick, grievously laments his wretched state (2–12). II. Reflecting on the sad lot of the city and exiles, he asks God, the always merciful one, to restore the people and city (13–23). III. Reverting again to his own affliction, he asks that God, who endures forever, will not call him from this life, until his days are done (24–29).

1 *A prayer of an afflicted man, when, exhausted, he pours out his griefs before the Lord.*

I 2 Lord, hear my prayer,
and bid my cry come to your throne.
3 O do not hide your face from me
on the day of my distress;
incline to me your ear;
when I invoke you, swiftly answer me.
4 Like smoke my days are vanishing;
my bones are as a burning fire.
5 Like dried-up grass, my heart is withering,
and I forget to eat my daily bread.
6 Because my groans are vehement
I am but skin and bones.
7 Like am I to a pelican within a wilderness,
or like an owl in ruined tower;
8 and sleepless I keep moaning through the night,

100:8. It was the custom for the king to pass judgment on offenders every morning at the gate of the city.

101:7, 8. The poet compares himself to solitude-loving birds which haunt desolate places. Their mournful cries can be heard during the night. Traditionally, the owl is thought to prefer ruins as a place of abode.

like to a bird forlorn upon the roof.
9 My foes insult me ceaselessly;
in furious rage, they use my name to imprecate.
10 Dust is the daily bread I eat;
my drink I mingle with my tears,
11 for in your bursts of wrath
you lifted me up, then threw me down.
12 My days are like to lengthening shades;
like grass, I wither away.

II 13 But you, O Lord, endure eternally;
your name endures from age to age.
14 Then rise; to Sion show your graciousness;
for time it is you pitied it; the hour has come indeed.
15 Your loyal servants love its very stones;
its ruin breaks their hearts.
16 The nations will revere your name, O Lord,
and all earth's kings your majesty,
17 as soon as the Lord has Sion built anew,
and in his glory has revealed himself;
18 and when he heeds the poor men's prayer,
and does not disregard their cry.

19 Let this be written for a future race,
and let a race yet to be born acclaim the Lord;
20 because the Lord looked from his shrine on high,
looked down from heaven upon the earth,
21 to hear the groans of captive men,
to free those doomed to death.
22 In Sion must the Lord's name be announced,
and in Jerusalem his praise,
23 soon as the nations and the kingdoms
congregate to serve the Lord.

101:9b. *they use my name to imprecate:* i.e., his foes use his name in formulas of cursing: "May the same things happen to you as happened to him." What this wretched plight is, is indicated in the next few verses.
101:11b. As one might lift high over his head a heavy weight and then angrily cast it down.
101:12. *lengthening shades:* the long shadows cast by the setting sun.
101:19. The verse means: let the blessings (cf. vv. 20, 21) which God has bestowed upon his people be recorded for the knowledge of posterity.

III ²⁴ He has worn out my strength midway;
  he has cut short my days.
 ²⁵ I say: "My God, O do not snatch me off midway, before my days
   are done;
  your years endure from age to age.
 ²⁶ You founded the earth when time began;
  and heaven is your handiwork;
 ²⁷ these run their course, but you endure;
  and, like a cloak, all things grow old.
  You change them like a cloak, and they are changed!
 ²⁸ But you remain the same: your years will never end.
 ²⁹ Your servants' sons will live in peace;
  their offspring will endure to worship you."

PSALM 102

Praises of God's Mercy

Great affection and tenderness characterize this psalm.
 I. After he has sung the praises of God (1, 2), the psalmist glories
in the mercy of God, which he himself has experienced (3–5). II.
He next tells of the blessings which God has extended to his people
(6–10). III. He extols the immensity of this divine mercy, compar-
ing the love of God with the smallness and weakness of men (11–
18). IV. He calls upon all men and the whole universe to render
praises to the Most High God (19–22).

 ¹ A psalm of David.

I O bless, my soul, the Lord;
  and all that is within me bless his holy name!
 ² O bless, my soul, the Lord;
  do not forget his blessings, each and all.
 ³ 'Tis he that pardons all your faults;
  that heals all your infirmities;
 ⁴ that saves your life from death;
  that crowns you with his mercy and his grace;

 101:24. The liberation of his people is taking so long that the psalmist's
strength is being exhausted. He thinks that he may die before the liberation
comes. Hence, in v. 25, he asks that he may not be taken off before his
days are done.

5 that fills your life with all good things.
Renewed by him, your youth is eaglelike.

II 6 The Lord does what is right and just,
sees justice done to all oppressed.
7 To Moses he revealed his ways,
to Israel's children all his deeds.
8 The Lord is merciful and kind,
to anger slow, and rich in clemency.
9 He is not finding fault perpetually,
nor does he bear a grudge for aye.
10 He does not deal with us according to our sins,
nor punish us according to our faults.

III 11 As heaven towers above the earth,
so toward his worshippers his mercy wins the day;
12 as far as Orient is from Occident,
so far does he remove from us our sins;
13 as sire is merciful to son,
so does the Lord show mercy to his worshipers.
14 He knows the stuff of which we are made,
and he remembers we are dust.
15 Man's days are like to grass;
like flower in field — so does he bloom:
16 the breeze has hardly brushed it — it is no more;
its very place no longer knows it!
17 The Lord's eternal mercy shields his worshipers eternally;
his justice shields their children's endless line,
18 if they observe his covenant, remember his
decrees, and keep them faithfully.

IV 19 The Lord has fixed his seat in heaven;
his kingship rules the universe.
20 O all his angels, bless the Lord;
you, mighty princes, carry out his orders
and obey his word!

102:5b. There was a belief that an old eagle became young again by some
change that took place in its plumage.
102:16. So fleeting is the memory of man that the very place where he
dwelt no longer remembers him.

21 O bless the Lord, all you, his hosts,
   his ministers, who carry out his will.
22 All you, his creatures, bless the Lord
   in every place of his domain!
   O bless, my soul, the Lord!

PSALM 103

Praise of God, the Creator

The psalmist, moved with admiration for God, the creator of all things, contemplates the universe, and everywhere in it, he finds evidences of one supreme maker and conserver. I. The heavens are his seat; the light, his mantle; the clouds, his chariot; the winds, his messengers (2–4). II. By his own power, God fixed and formed the land (5–9). III. The waters of the rivers and the rains he gave, in order that verdure might spring up, which men could use for sustenance and animals for dwelling places (10–18). IV. The sun and moon, created by God, limit for man and beast the time of their activities (19–23). V. The sea, with its small creatures and its monsters, is the work of God (24–26). VI. The beginning and end of all life depends upon his will (27–30). VII. It is proper for all good men to praise this benign and powerful God; let sinners, however, no longer encumber the earth (31–35).

I   1 O bless, my soul, the Lord!
      O Lord, my God, you are exceeding great!
      Magnificence and beauty are your robes:
    2 light, as a raiment, wraps you round.
      You spread the heavens — curtainlike;
    3 above high waters you have built your halls;
      the clouds you make your chariot,
      you ride upon the wings of wind.
    4 The storms you make your messengers,
      the fiery bolts your ministers.

II 5 Upon its base you made the earth secure,
      and it shall never lose stability.

103:3. *above high waters:* the ancient Hebrews conceived of a great reservoir of waters (this was the source of rain) as existing above the firmament (cf. Gen. 1:7; Pss. 28:3; 148:4). Above this reservoir God built his secret dwelling place.

103:5. *Upon its base:* the earth is compared to a splendid edifice reared on a solid foundation.

⁶ You wrapped the ocean round it as a cloak.
The waters on the mountains poised:
⁷ you sternly spoke: they fled away;
you thundered: they were terrified.
⁸ The mountains rose; the valleys sank
down to the place you had assigned to them;
⁹ you set a bound they might not cross,
lest they should cover up the earth again.

III   ¹⁰ The springs you bid to empty into streams
that flow between the mountainsides;
¹¹ they furnish drink to every ranging beast;
wild asses slake their thirst in them.
¹² And on their banks dwell birds that roam the air;
among the boughs they warble out their songs.
¹³ You dew the mountains from your reservoirs;
in fruit which you produce the earth abounds.
¹⁴ You sprout the grass to feed the kine,
and plants, to serve the needs of man.
Thus from the earth he draws his daily bread,
¹⁵ and wine to cheer his heart,
and oil to light his face,
and bread to make him hale and strong.
¹⁶ The Lord's own trees — they draw their fill —
the cedars which you planted on Mount Lebanon.
¹⁷ There birds set up their nests;
firs are the haunts of storks;
¹⁸ the mountain crags give cover to gazelles;
hedgehogs feel safe in rocky caves.

IV   ¹⁹ You made the moon to mark the seasons;
the sun knows well its setting time.
²⁰ You make the dark: then comes the night,
and in it beasts of forests roam.
²¹ The cubs of lions roar for prey,
and ask of God their food;

103:8. At God's command the ocean receded so that the mountains
and valleys appeared.
103:9. *you set a bound*: i.e., for the waters of the ocean (v. 6).

22 at sunrise they slink back again,
and in their lairs lie down for rest.

23 Then man goes forth to do his work,
and plies his task till evening comes.

V 24 How many are the things you do, O Lord!
With wisdom you accomplish everything!
And with your creatures teems the earth:

25 there is the ocean, vast and stretching far;
therein are creeping things past numbering,
small animals as well as great;

26 therein sea monsters move about —
Leviathan, which you have made to sport in it.

VI 27 All are expecting you
to give them food at the appointed time.

28 You offer it: they gather it;
you open your hand: they take their fill of what is good;

29 you hide your face: they are alarmed;
you take their breath away: they die,
and back they go unto the dust they are;

30 you send your spirit forth: they are created,
and you renew the face of the earth.

VII 31 May the glory of the Lord forever last!
And may the Lord have joy in all his works!

32 A frown of his: the earth begins to quake;
a touch of his: the mountains belch forth smoke!

33 As long as I live will I sing to the Lord,
and hymn the praise of my God as long as I last.

34 May he be pleased with my poor utterance:
for me, I will rejoice in the Lord.

35 Let sinners perish from the earth,
and let the godless be no more!
O bless, my soul, the Lord! Alleluia!

103:26b. *Leviathan:* the crocodile. In pagan mythology, Leviathan was a monster that fought with the gods. To the psalmist, however, it is the huge creature created by God to play in his ocean.

103:30. The spirit of God is the cause of all life, and in a special manner, that of man (cf. Gen. 2:7).

103:35. Sin is the only jarring note in God's creation. It is sin that angers God (v. 32). Hence the psalmist wishes that sinners may perish from the earth.

PSALM 104

God's Promises to Abraham Are Fulfilled

This psalm, as do Psalms 77, 105, 106, 135, gives a history of the
Israelites; its purpose is to show the kindness and justice of God's
providence. I. The psalmist urges all men to honor the works of
God (1–7). II. He recalls the pact entered into with the patriarchs,
and the promises made by God that the people would possess the
land of Chanaan (8–11). III. God protected the patriarchs (12–15).
IV. The life of Joseph is given in brief outline (16–22). V. Then
follows an account of the Israelites' going into Egypt (23, 24). VI.
The psalmist recounts the charge given to Moses and Aaron (25–
27). VII. He describes the Egyptian plagues (28–38). VIII. He
enumerates the miracles that were performed during the return from
Egypt and in the desert (39–43). IX. Finally, the psalmist concludes
by showing that the Israelites took possession of the land of the
Chanaanites, which had been promised them (44, 45).

I   1   O hymn the Lord; acclaim his name;
       make known his deeds among the nations!
   2   Sing and play the harp to honor him;
       tell all his wondrous deeds!
   3   And glory in his holy name;
       may every heart that seeks the Lord rejoice!
   4   Consider well the Lord and all his might;
       and ever seek his kindly face.
   5   Recall the wonders he has done,
       his miracles, the judgments he pronounced,
   6   O children of his servant Abraham,
       O sons of Jacob, his elect!
   7   He is the Lord our God;
       throughout the world his judgments are in force.

II   8   He is forever mindful of his covenant —
       the pledge he for a thousand ages gave,
   9   the covenant he struck for Abraham,
       the oath he made to Isaac,
   10   the firm decree he ratified for Jacob,
       the covenant he struck for Israel,

11 when he declared: "To you I give the land of Chanaan
  to be your own hereditary lot."

III 12 When they in number were but few —
  a little band of strangers in that land —
13 and wandered on from tribe to tribe,
  from a kingdom here to a people there,
14 he allowed no man to press them hard,
  and for their sake reproved the kings:
15 "Lay not your hand on my anointed ones,
  and to my prophets do no harm."

IV 16 And then he bade a famine come upon the land,
  and he withheld their whole supply of bread.
17 Before them he had sent a man:
  Joseph, who was sold to slavery.
18 His feet were bound with chains;
  an iron band lay round his neck,
19 till his prediction was fulfilled
  and the Lord's word vindicated him.
20 The king, the ruler of the land,
  had him released and set him free.
21 And he appointed him the master of his house,
  to be the Lord of his possessions, one and all,
22 to punish all his noblemen at his own will,
  and teach his old men wisdom's lore.

V 23 Then Israel entered into Egypt,
  and Jacob was an alien in the land of Cham.
24 He multiplied his race exceedingly,
  and made it stronger than its foes.

VI 25 He turned the people's hearts to hate his race
  and with his servants deal deceitfully.
26 And then he sent his servant Moses,
  and Aaron, his own chosen one;
27 and in their midst they worked his miracles,
  his wonders in the land of Cham.

104:15. *anointed ones*: the prophets who were consecrated to God in a special way and received revelations from him.
104:23b. Cham is another name for Egypt (cf. Gen. 10:16).
104:25. *the people's hearts*: sc., the hearts of the Egyptians.

VII ²⁸ Darkness he sent; there was dense night;
    and yet, they set at nought his words!
 ²⁹ He turned their waters into blood,
    and killed their fish.
 ³⁰ Their country swarmed with frogs,
    which even filled the chambers of their kings.
 ³¹ He spoke the word: on came a swarm of flies,
    and gnats filled every corner of their land.

 ³² For rain he gave them hail
    and flaming fire throughout their land.
 ³³ He killed their fig trees and their vines,
    and in their country rent the trees.
 ³⁴ He spoke again: the locusts came,
    and grasshoppers past all numbering;
 ³⁵ and all the herbage they devoured within the land,
    devoured the fruit trees in the fields.
 ³⁶ And all the first-born in the land he slew,
    the first fruits of their loins.
 ³⁷ He led them forth, enriched with silver and with gold;
    there was no weakling in their clans.
 ³⁸ And glad was Egypt they were gone,
    for dread of them had overtaken it.

VIII ³⁹ He spread a cloud to shelter them,
    and gave them fire for light throughout the night.
 ⁴⁰ They begged: he brought a flock of quail,
    and sated them with heaven's bread.
 ⁴¹ He cleft the rock, and water flowed,
    which through the desert ran in streams.
 ⁴² For he was mindful of his holy word,
    which he had given to his servant Abraham.
 ⁴³ And so he led his people forth with joy,
    and his elect with jubilee.

104:28–38. Here, as in Ps. 77:44–51, the plagues of Egypt are ordered and described with some poetical liberty.

104:37. Israel went forth from Egypt like a victorious army, rich in spoils and in which there were no weak or puny privates. If, however, the parallelism is to be preserved, weakling might better be rendered as "poor man," or "needy one."

IX **44** He gave to them the heathen lands;
          they took possession of the nations' wealth,
     45 that they might cherish his commands,
          and make his laws their own, Alleluia!

PSALM 105

The Sins of an Ungrateful People;
Their Chastisements

This psalm, too, narrates the history of the Israelite people; it tells
how frequent and monstrous was their ingratitude to God. In the
poem (A) the psalmist exhorts them to praise the mercy and power
of God (1–5); then (B) he enumerates in the following eight sections eight times that the Israelites lapsed in their duties toward
God. I. He begins with the sins their fathers committed in Egypt
and at the time of the Exodus; these sins were all the more grave
because God had so wonderfully freed them from their enemies'
grip (6–12). II. Forgetful of these blessings, they sinned again by
concupiscence (13–15). III. They further offended God by rebellion
(16–18). IV. They made a golden calf (19–23). V. They spurned
the promised land (24–27). VI. They sacrificed to Beelphegor (28–
31). VII. They led Moses himself into sinning (32, 33). VIII. When
they entered Palestine, they did not exterminate the Chanaanites
there, but adored the false gods worshiped in this land, and sacrificed their own sons to them (34–39). (C) Hence God handed them
over into the hands of the enemy (40–42). But, although they
sinned again and again, God, mindful of his pact, spared them (43–
46). The psalm concludes with prayers with which the return from
exile is sought (47). The last verse (48) is the conclusion of Book
IV of the psalms.

   1 *Alleluia.*

A   O hymn the Lord, for he is kind;
          his mercy lasts eternally.
     2 Who can recount the deeds of might, wrought by the Lord,
          or publish all his claims to praise?
     3 O well for those who keep the laws
          and always do the right.

104:44. *heathen lands:* i.e., Palestine, which earlier had been inhabited by
various pagan tribes.

4 Remember me, O Lord, kind to your people as you are,
and visit me to give me help.
5 O let me taste the happiness of your elect,
take pleasure in your people's joy,
and share the glory with your heritage.

B I 6 Yes, like our fathers we have sinned;
we have done wrong; we acted impiously.
7 Our ancestors in Egypt paid
no heed to all your wondrous deeds.
They were not mindful of your many kindnesses,
and they defied the Most High God at the Red Sea's marge.
8 Yet for his name's sake he delivered them
to manifest his might.
9 The Red Sea he rebuked; dried up it was!
He led them through the waves as o'er dry land;
10 he rescued them from haters' hands,
and freed them from the enemies' grip.
11 The waters buried all their foes:
not one of them was left alive.
12 Then they believed his words;
and how they sang his praise!

II 13 But quickly they forgot his deeds,
and in his wisdom put no trust;
14 for in the desert they indulged their lust,
and in the wilderness they tempted God.
15 He granted their request,
but sent on them a fell disease.

III 16 They envied Moses in the camp;
they envied Aaron, God's holy one.
17 The earth then yawned and swallowed Dathan,
and buried all Abiron's band.
18 Then fire broke out to kill their company;
a flame consumed the wicked men.

IV 19 They made a calf in Horeb and
adored the idol made of molten gold.

105:16–18. Cf. Num. 16.

20 O what exchange! The image of a hay-consuming ox
replaced the glory of the race!
21 The God who saved them — they forgot,
him who in Egypt once had portents wrought,
22 who in the land of Cham did wondrous things,
and at the Red Sea, miracles!
23 And then he thought to make away with them,
had not his chosen servant Moses
appealed to him and warded off his wrath,
lest they should be destroyed.

V 24 They then disdained the longed-for land,
and failed to trust his word.
25 They murmured in their tents,
and disobeyed the Lord.
26 And with uplifted hand he swore to them
that he would in the desert lay them low,
27 disperse their children 'mongst the nations,
and scatter them throughout the world.

VI 28 They gave allegiance to Beelphegor,
and ate the sacrifices offered to dead gods.
29 And they provoked him by their crimes,
and then a plague came down on them.
30 But Phinees arose and executed punishment;
and the plague was stopped.
31 His action was adjudged a meritorious deed for him,
for age on age, forever and for aye.

VII 32 They irritated him at the Meriba Springs,
and it went ill with Moses on account of them:
33 they had embittered him,
and he was inconsiderate in speech.

105:20b. God was the Glory of Israel. This invisible, spiritual God they
exchanged for the likeness of an animal.
105:24. They spurned the pleasant land of Chanaan, even after their
spies had returned with favorable reports on it (cf. Num. 14).
105:28. They sinned by worshiping *Beelphegor*, one of the deities of the
Moabites (cf. Num. 25:2).
105:32, 33. It went ill with Moses, since, as a punishment, he was pro-
hibited from entering into the promised land (cf. Num. 20:1–13).

VIII ³⁴ They did not extirpate the heathen tribes
         as the Lord had bidden them.
     ³⁵ And with the heathens they held intercourse,
         and learnt their ways of life.
     ³⁶ They idolized their graven images,
         and these became a snare to them.
     ³⁷ They sacrificed their sons
         and daughters to the demon gods;
     ³⁸ and shed blood that was innocent,
         their sons' and daughters' blood,
         whom they to Chanaan's idols sacrificed.
         The land was fouled by gore;
     ³⁹ they were contaminated by their practices,
         and by their crimes they proved adulterous.

C   ⁴⁰ The fury of the Lord flared up against his race,
         and he abhorred his heritage;
     ⁴¹ he gave them over to the heathen tribes;
         and men that hated them ruled over them.
     ⁴² Their enemies tormented them;
         their mighty hand bore down on them.
     ⁴³ He oftentimes delivered them,
         but they provoked him with their schemes,
         and owing to their sins they were laid low.
     ⁴⁴ And yet he kindly looked on their afflicted state,
         as often as he heard their cry;
     ⁴⁵ and for their sake he bore in mind his covenant,
         and in surpassing mercy he relented.
     ⁴⁶ And mercy, too, he won for them
         from all that held them in captivity.
     ⁴⁷ Save us, O Lord, our God,
         and gather us from 'mongst the heathen tribes,
         that we may celebrate your holy name,
         and glory in your praise.

     ⁴⁸ Blessed be the Lord, the God of Israel;
         as from eternity, so shall it be eternally!
         Let all the people say: "So be it! Alleluia!"

    105:39b. *adulterous*: this term is often used by the prophets as applied to
the worship of false gods.

BOOK 5: Psalms 106-150

PSALM 106

Thanksgiving for Deliverance From Perils

The psalm begins with a prologue (1–3) in which those who have been freed from exile are told to thank God. The psalm has two parts: the first (A: 4–32) describes the liberation of the Israelites from four perils. I. Wandering in the desert and suffering from starvation there, they were given their fill of food (4–9). II. Those who had been imprisoned were set free (10–16). III. The seriously ill were cured (17–22). IV. Those navigating the sea were saved from shipwreck by storm and were led to the safety of a port (23–32).

In the second part (B: 33–43), there is a description of how the providence of God changed fertile regions into deserts, and desert lands into fertile fields, where he settled the Israelites and blessed and multiplied their families (33–41). In an epilogue (42, 43) the psalmist advises all the people to meditate well on these blessings which God gave them.

1 O hymn the Lord, for he is kind;
his mercy lasts eternally.

2 Let all delivered by the Lord join in this song —
whom he delivered from the foe,

3 and gathered in from every land,
both east and west, both north and south.

A I 4 They wandered in a lonely wilderness,
and did not find a fitting place to live;

5 they suffered hunger, suffered thirst;
their very life was ebbing out.

6 *To the Lord they cried in their distress,
and from their straits he rescued them.*

7 He led them on by the right path,
that they might find a fitting place to live.

8 *O let them thank the Lord for all his kindliness,
and for his wondrous dealings with the sons of men.*

9 He satisfied the starving souls,
and showered good things on the hungry multitude.

II 10 They sat in darkness and in gloom,

106:10, 11. They were put into prison as a punishment for their grievous sins, just as the exile itself was a punishment for sin.

173

in misery clad, and iron-bound;
11 they had rebelled against the words of God,
the Most High's counsel they despised.
12 He humbled them, and grief gnawed at their hearts;
they fainted: there was none to help.
13 *To the Lord they cried in their distress,*
and from their straits he rescued them.
14 He led them forth from darkness and from gloom,
and broke their chains asunder.
15 *O let them thank the Lord for all his kindliness,*
and for his wondrous dealings with the sons of men:
16 he burst the bronzen gates,
and broke the iron bars.

III 17 When they were ill because of their iniquities,
afflicted for their crimes,
18 and felt disgust for every kind of food,
and neared the gates of death,
19 *to the Lord they cried in their distress,*
and from their straits he rescued them.
20 And his command went forth to make them well
and snatch them from the grave.
21 *O let them thank the Lord for all his kindliness,*
and for his wondrous dealings with the sons of men.
22 And let them sacrifice to voice their thanks,
and tell with joy whatever he has done.

IV 23 Down to the sea some went to sail
and traffic over seas;
24 and then these witnessed what the Lord can do,
his wondrous deeds upon the main.
25 He spoke; he roused a stormy wind,
and tossed the waves aloft.
26 Sky-high they mounted, then sank into the deep!
O how their human spirits fainted in their plight!
27 They reeled and staggered just like drunken men,

106:25–27. This description of the storm is noteworthy, especially since the Hebrews were not a seagoing people, and hence, had little knowledge of marine phenomena.

and all their seamanship was gone!
28 Yet, to the Lord they cried in their distress,
and from their straits he rescued them.
29 He quelled the storm down to a gentle breeze —
and silent were the sea's waves.
30 How they rejoiced when these were quiet!
He led them safely to the longed-for port.
31 O let them thank the Lord for all his kindliness,
and for his wondrous dealings with the sons of men.
32 And let them sing his praise at people's gatherings;
let them exalt him when the elders meet.

33 He changed the rivers into desert land,
a land of springs into a thirsty ground;
34 a fertile land into a salty waste,
because of the sins of those who dwell therein.
35 He changed a desert into a sheet of water,
and a dry waste into a land of springs.
36 And there he settled the hungry multitude;
and there they built a fitting place to dwell.
37 They sowed the fields and planted vines,
and thus obtained an ample crop.
38 He blessed them, and they multiplied exceedingly,
and cattle in abundance he bestowed on them.
39 Brought low they were, in numbers few,
oppressed by ills and misery;
40 but he who pours contempt on princely men
and makes them stray through trackless wastes,
41 raised up the needy from their misery,
and multiplied their families like flocks.

42 On seeing this, the true of heart exult;
all malice shuts its mouth.
43 Where is the wise man that observes these things,
and duly weighs the mercies of the Lord?

106:32. It was the custom for the elders to meet at the gate of the city
to pass judgment on cases brought to them (cf. Ruth 4:1 ff.).
106:33–41. These verses recount the aid God gave to the Israelites when
they were returning from exile and were establishing themselves in Palestine.

Psalm 107

Praise of God and a Petition for His Aid in War

This psalm is made up of verses taken from Psalm 56 (8–12) and Psalm 59 (7–14). I. In the first part, the psalmist expresses his unshaken trust in God. It is this trust which spurs him on to plead for victory (2–7). II. In the second part, the promise of God is recalled (8–10) and his help implored (11–14).

1 A song. A psalm of David.

I 2 My heart is strong, O Lord; my heart is strong;
with song and lyre I jubilate.
Awake, my soul!
3 Awaken, song and lyre!
I will awake the dawn!
4 Among the peoples will I praise you, Lord;
among the nations sing a song to you!
5 As high as heaven is your kindliness,
high as the clouds your faithfulness!
6 O show yourself supreme in heaven, God;
and may your glory shine on all the earth!
7 To free your loved ones
hear our prayers and help with your right hand.

II 8 And God has spoken in his holy shrine:
"With joy will I divide up Sichem,
and parcel out the Succoth vale.
9 Mine is the land of Galaad, mine is Manasses' land;
the helmet of my head is Ephraim, and Juda is my staff;
10 Moab shall be my washing bowl;
on Edom will I set my heel,
and triumph o'er Philistia."
11 Who is to lead me to the mighty citadel?
Who is to lead me on to Edom?
12 Will not you, O God, who have discarded us,
not you, O God, who with our hosts no longer march?

107:8–14. Cf. Ps. 59, footnotes.
107:12. This verse expresses confident hope in God, even though he has seemingly abandoned his people.

13 Then give us help against the foe,
for vain is any help of man.
14 With God's help we will bravely act;
'tis he will trample on your foes.

PSALM 108

Against Unjust and Relentless Enemies

I. The psalm begins with a prayer against unjust and treacherous foes (1b–5). II. Then various curses are uttered against a particular enemy (6–19): that he may always be judged guilty (6, 7); that he may die prematurely and leave his dependents in misery (8–10); that he may lose his prosperity and all his riches (11); that he may be deprived of the kindliness of neighbors (12); that his descendants may become extinct and that he himself will have to atone for the sins of his ancestors (13–15); that his punishment will be in exact retaliation for the evil he has done (16–19). III. The psalmist urgently asks God that he may be freed from the overwhelming evils with which he is afflicted, and that his enemies may be put to shame (20–31).

As regards the imprecations expressed in this and some other psalms, it should be noted that the law of retaliation (lex talionis) obtained in the Old Testament (Exod. 21:12; 23–25; Lev. 24:17–21) and that punishments, in general, were then much more severe than those meted out in our times. Since, moreover, the psalmist wrote in a poetical strain, these metaphors are not to be taken in an entirely literal sense. Further, the psalmist is concerned not only with his own private affairs, when he speaks against his enemies, but also with a defense of God. The psalmist is attacked by foes precisely because he is a faithful observer of God's commands.

1 To the choirmaster. A psalm of David.

I God, shield of my good name, speak out!
2 With wicked and deceitful lips they cry me down;
they speak to me with lying tongues;
3 with hateful speech they buzz around me,
and, unprovoked, they combat me.
4 My love they match with accusations:
but I — I prayed!
5 With ill for good they have requited me,
with hatred for my love.

II   6   Then raise a wicked man to combat him
      and stand accuser at his right.
   7   When he is judged, let him come out condemned,
      and may his plea be all in vain.
   8   His days — may they be few;
      his office — someone else succeed to it!
   9   His children — be they fatherless;
      his wife — may she be husbandless.
   10   His sons — let them unstably roam and beg,
      ejected from their ruined homes.
   11   May usurers lie in wait for all his property,
      and strangers plunder what his labor earned.
   12   May no one show him any kindnesses;
      may no one pity to his orphans show.
   13   May his posterity become extinct;
      his name be blotted out within another generation.
   14   His fathers' sins be all remembered by the Lord;
      may not his mother's sins be blotted out:
   15   may the Lord at all times think of them!
      May he in every place eradicate their memory!
   16   For he never thought of showing kindliness,
      but persecuted the poor and needy man,
      the one who suffered grief, and sought to take his life.
   17   Of malediction he was fond — may it now fall on him;
      he slighted benediction — be it withheld from him.
   18   And malediction clothe him like a cloak;
      like water, penetrate his inmost soul;
      like oil, his every bone.
   19   Be it a robe that wraps him round,
      a cincture always girdling him.

III   20   This be the Lord's reward for my accusers,
      for those whose speech abuses me.

108:6. See Zach. 3:1, where there is an instance of an accuser standing at the right hand of the accused high priest, to be his adversary.

108:15b. The poet asks that the very memory of the whole line, both ancestors and posterity, be destroyed.

108:19. The wicked man developed the habit of cursing. Therefore, let it ever cling to him like a garment, bind him about like a girdle.

21 But you, Lord God, deal with me for your name's sake;
   since you are kind and merciful, deliver me.
22 I am a poor and wretched man;
   my inmost heart is sore distressed.
23 Like a declining shade, I fade away;
   I vanish like a locust on the wing.
24 Because I fast, my knees are quaking;
   my body shrinks and wastes away.
25 A byword am I now to them;
   at sight of me, they shake their heads.
26 Help me, O Lord, my God;
   in your abounding kindliness deliver me.
27 O let them know this is your work —
   that you, O Lord, have accomplished this.
28 If you but bless me, let them curse.
   May my assailants be discomfited,
   but may your servant leap with joy.
29 Let my accusers don the robe of shame;
   and may confusion, like a garment, wrap them round.
30 But I will loudly hymn the Lord,
   and praise him in the midst of throngs;
31 because he stands at the poor man's right,
   securing him from men that are unjust.

PSALM 109

The Messias, Priest, King, Victor

I. The psalm foretells the royal dignity that the Messias will enjoy, a dignity which was conferred upon him by God and has its source in his divine origin (1–3). II. It foretells also his sacerdotal dignity (4) and III. the ultimate victory that he will have over all his enemies (5–7).

1 A psalm of David.

I   The Lord said to my Lord: "Sit on my right
until I make your foes the footstool of your feet."

² Your mighty sceptre the Lord from Sion will extend:
"Hold sway amidst your enemies;

³ princedom was yours — the day you were in holy splendor born;
before the morning star, like dew, have I begotten you."

II   ⁴ The Lord has sworn and he shall never rue it:
"You are a priest for aye according to the pattern of Melchisedech."

III   ⁵ The Lord is on your right;
he will, upon the day of wrath, crush kings;

⁶ the nations he will judge, and pile up corpse on corpse;
he will crush heads far and wide through the land.

⁷ From wayside torrents he will drink,
and therefore lift his head.

PSALM 110

God's Splendid Works in Israel

This is an alphabetical psalm (see the introduction to Psalm 9).
The following thoughts are presented: all the works of God are great
and worthy of profound meditation (2, 3); God himself provides
that the memory of his great works shall continue among his people,
whether by tradition or feasts (4). Chief among the works of God,
the psalmist enumerates the gift of manna in the desert (5), the
possession of the land of Chanaan (6), the enactment of firm, stable,
and just laws (7, 8), the freeing of his people from various dangers
and his constant remembrance of the pact he had made with them
(9). Hence, the highest wisdom is to fear God, that is, to cherish
him with reverence (10).

109:4b. *according to the pattern of Melchisedech:* i.e., his priesthood is a
true one, as was that of Melchisedech, and not merely a levitical priesthood as
was that of the sons of Aaron (cf. Hebr. 7:11–28). Melchisedech was a true
priest who offered sacrifice of bread and wine.

109:5. *on your right:* to give you aid in battle with rebellious kings.

109:6. *pile up corpse on corpse:* a metaphor to indicate that the battles
will be fierce and bloody.

109:7. *From wayside torrents he will drink:* the Messias, fatigued by the
battle, restores his strength by a draught from a torrent, in order that he
may go on to new victories. Metaphorically, this can be explained thus: the
Messias will always have divine aid on his way, which will be a help to him
to bear up and go on to victory.

1 *Alleluia.*

I hymn the Lord with all my heart
whene'er the saints in private or in public meet.
2 Great are the doings of the Lord,
and deeply to be scanned by all that love him!
3 His work is all magnificence, all majesty;
his justice lasts eternally.
4 He made his wondrous actions worth remembering;
the Lord is kind and merciful.
5 To all his worshipers he gave to eat;
eternally he will be mindful of his covenant.
6 The power he wields he manifested to his people
by giving them possession of the heathen lands.
7 Fidelity and justice mark whate'er he does,
and firmly grounded are his laws,
8 secured to last for ages and eternity,
all firmly fixed and fair.
9 He sent redemption to his chosen race,
and made his covenant to last eternally.
All-worshipful and holy is his name.
10 The sum of wisdom is "fear of the Lord";
and well-advised are all who practice it.
Worthy of praise is he eternally.

Psalm 111

The Happiness of a Good Man

This psalm, like the preceding one, is alphabetical. Its subject is the
life that a good man leads and the happiness that follows from it.
The psalm lauds the just man's fidelity to the laws of God (1), his
munificence (3, 9), the mercy with which he aids others (4, 5), his
justice in handling of his own affairs (5).

The rewards of such a good life are: the influence that the good
man and his offspring have over others (2, 9), riches (3), safety
from perils (6, 7), a soul filled with confidence (8), the lasting
remembrance men will have of him (6). Wicked men will be
enraged at the sight of him, but their fury will be in vain (10).

The rewards promised are, after the manner of the Old Testament,
of this world; for a Christian, such things are raised to a higher
order.

1 *Alleluia.*

Well for the man who fears the Lord,
and in his laws takes great delight.
2 Mighty in the land is his posterity;
the children of the saints are blest.
3 And in his house there is abundant wealth;
ever he has the means of being bountiful.
4 On gloomy days he rises as a light to pious souls;
for he is kind and merciful and just.
5 Well for the man who is compassionate and lends,
who is in all his dealings fair and square.
6 He will not lose his footing in eternity;
a good man is remembered evermore.
7 Of ill report he has no fear;
his heart is stout and trusting in the Lord.
8 His heart is steadfast; without fear he waits
till he can see his foes discomfited.
9 He showers his gifts upon the poor;
ever he has the means of being bountiful.
His might and glory are a theme for song.
10 The sinner sees it, and he is enraged;
he grinds his teeth and pines away.
The sinners' wish shall never be fulfilled.

Psalm 112

Praise of the All-High and All-Merciful God

I. Let true servants of the Lord praise him at all times and in all places (1–3). II. The Lord's might excels both heaven and earth (4–6). III. He is kindly to the lowly and those held in contempt by men (7–9).

111:3. The just man will so use his wealth that he will always have the means of being generous to others.

111:4. The good man is like a light to those suffering from the darkness of adversity and troubles.

111:10. Sinners are angry and envious at the sight of blessings showered on virtuous men, but their envy is futile.

1 *Alleluia.*

I   Praise, you servants of the Lord,
     O praise the name of the Lord.
2   The Lord's name be blest
     both now and in eternity.
3   From the rising to the setting sun
     the name of the Lord be praised.

II   4 Supreme above all nations is the Lord;
     his glory is above the firmament.
5   Who is like the Lord our God,
     who thrones on high
6   and sees what is below, both in the heavens and on earth!

II   7 He lifts the helpless from the dust,
     and from the dunghill raises up the poor,
8   and places them with princes,
     the princes of his chosen race.
9   He makes the barren woman rule a home,
     a mother joying in her offspring.

PSALM 113A

The Marvels Worked by God During the Exodus

In this short song, the psalmist describes how Israel became the
people of God (1, 2), and how nature was affected when God led
his people from Egypt (3, 4). The psalmist, as if mystified, asks
nature why it is so moved (5, 6); but before nature can respond,
he himself states that the very earth should tremble when God so
splendidly manifests his omnipotence (7, 8).

1 *Alleluia.*

When Israel went forth from Egypt —
the house of Jacob from a race of alien tongue —
2 Juda became his holy place,
his kingdom Israel.

112:6. God is represented as sitting on a throne so high that he must
look down to see both heaven and earth.

112:9. Sterility was looked upon as a curse and a punishment (cf. Gen.
16:4, 5; 1 Sam. 7–11; 2, 5).

3 The sea looked up and fled;
   the Jordan backward rolled;
4 the mountains frisked like rams;
   the hills like little lambs!
5 What ails you, sea, that you should flee?
   What ails you, Jordan, that you should backward roll?
6 Why, mountains, do you frisk like rams;
   why, hills, like little lambs?

7 Tremble in the presence of the Lord, O earth,
   in the presence of Jacob's God,
8 who turned a rock into a water well,
   a flint rock to a gushing spring!

PSALM 113B

Greatness and Goodness of the True God

I. The omnipotent God dwells in heaven; he alone is worthy of praise (1–3). II. The idols worshiped by the Gentiles are vain and impotent things (4–8). III. Hence, all Israel trusts in the true God; he it is that blesses them (9–18).

I 1 No, not to us, Lord, not to us:
     but to your name give glory,
     in honor of your mercy, of your faithfulness.
   2 Why should the Gentiles say:
     "Where is their God?"
   3 Our God — he is in heaven.
     All that he willed he made!

113:3, 4. The miracles performed at the crossing of the Red Sea and the Jordan and at Mount Sinai are presented in a dramatic way.

113:8. The psalmist recalls the miracle of the water as worked in the desert (Exod. 17:6 and Num. 20:11) to show that nothing is beyond the power of God.

113B:1. This psalm was apparently written at the time of the exile when the Gentiles held the Israelites and God in contempt. It might seem, the psalmist thinks, that God himself had been conquered by the gods of the Gentiles. Hence he calls upon God to take care of his own honor, for his mercy's, his truth's sake.

II   4 Their idols are but silver and gold,
     the work of human hands.
    5 They have a mouth, but do not speak;
     and they have eyes, but do not see;
    6 and they have ears, but do not hear;
     they have a nose, but do not smell;
    7 and they have hands, but do not feel;
     and they have feet, but do not walk;
     no sound they utter with their throat.
    8 Like them are all that fashion them,
     and everyone that trusts in them.

III   9 The house of Israel trusts in the Lord;
     their helper and their shield is he.
   10 The house of Aaron trusts in the Lord;
     their helper and their shield is he.
   11 All those who fear the Lord trust in the Lord;
     their helper and their shield is he.
   12 The Lord remembers us
     and blesses us;
     he blesses the house of Israel;
     he blesses Aaron's house.
   13 He blesses all that fear the Lord,
     the small ones and the great.
   14 The Lord will multiply you all —
     you and your sons.
   15 A blessing on you from the Lord,
     who made both heaven and earth.
   16 Heaven is the heaven of the Lord;
     the earth he has assigned to humankind.
   17 'Tis not the dead that praise the Lord,
     or any that descend to hell.
   18 But we — we bless the Lord,
     both now and in eternity.

113B:17, 18. Since those in hell can no longer praise God (cf. Pss. 6:6; 29:10; 87:11), it is the duty of the living, here on earth, to praise him.

Psalms 114 and 115
Thanksgiving of a Man Saved From Death

Since the thought and language of these two psalms are similar, many authorities hold that they form one song, of which the first part (A) deals with the love of God (cf. v. 1); the second (B), with confidence in him (v. 1).

A. In the first part (Ps. 114) the psalmist is pictured as freed from serious danger to his life (3, 8). I. He describes the peril which had threatened him and the prayers he had uttered (1–4). II. Now saved, and remembering God's mercy, he bids his soul be calm (5–9). B. In the second part (Ps. 115), the psalmist states that he puts his trust in God alone rather than in men (1, 2) and, rejoicing, he offers sacrifices of praise (3–10).

Psalm 114

¹ *Alleluia.*

A I I loved the Lord, because he heard
my pleading voice,
² and he inclined his ear to me
the day I called on him.
³ The ropes of death had coiled me round;
the snares of hell had seized on me:
to grief and pangs I was a prey.
⁴ Then I invoked the name of the Lord:
"Lord, save my life!"

II ⁵ Kind is the Lord and just;
our God is merciful.
⁶ The Lord guards simple souls:
I was in misery, and he delivered me.
⁷ Return, my soul, to your tranquillity:
the Lord has kindly dealt with you.
⁸ He saved my life from death,
my eyes from tears, and from a lapse my feet.
⁹ Now will I walk in the sight of the Lord
and in the land of the living.

114:3. Cf. Ps. 17:5, 6.
114:9. Cf. Ps. 55:14. Preserved from death, he will enjoy this life.

PSALM 115

B   1 I trusted — even when I said:
        "I am afflicted grievously!"
      2 I also said in my dismay:
         "No mortal is dependable!"
      3 How, then, shall I requite the Lord
         for all that he has granted me?
      4 In thanks for health received I take the cup
         and will invoke the name of the Lord:
      5 my vows will I pay to the Lord
         when all his people meet.
      6 No trifle, in the Lord's own reckoning,
         is the death of his saints!
      7 And since I am your servant, Lord,
         your servant, and your servant maid's own son,
         you have struck my bonds from me.
      8 And now I offer you a sacrifice to voice my praise,
         and I invoke the name of the Lord.
      9 My vows will I pay to the Lord
         when all his people meet
     10 within the courts of the house of the Lord,
         aye, in your very heart, Jerusalem!

115:4. The cup is the chalice with which the sacrifice of libation was offered in thanksgiving for blessings received. In offering the sacrifice, the name of the Lord was invoked.

115:6. *No trifle*, etc.: i.e., the life of the saints is a thing of great value; hence the Lord does not readily permit the death of good men, among whom is the psalmist (cf. v. 7).

115:7b. *your servant maid's own son:* I am your servant, not only by my own profession, but by my origin and stock.

PSALM 116

Hymn of Praise and Thanksgiving

The psalmist calls upon all peoples to sing the glory of God. It is, however, only in the kingdom of the Messias that this invitation will receive its full response (cf. Rom. 15:9–11).

1   *Alleluia.*

Now praise the Lord, O nations all;
proclaim his glory, peoples all!
2   For of his mercy toward us he has given fresh and mighty proofs:
the Lord's fidelity endures eternally.

PSALM 117

Thanksgiving for the Nation's Safety

This song is written in a joyful and dramatic strain. It seems to have been sung in the solemn entry to the temple, probably by many choristers, and very likely on the feast of the Tabernacles (cf. vv. 15, 27).

The psalmist begins (A) with a call to a general thanksgiving (1–4). Then (B) he tells of the harassing danger from which he had been rescued (5–18). I. In the midst of his trouble, he called upon God, the good God in whom all trust should be placed (5–9). II. When his enemies were pressing from all sides, the Lord preserved him in safety (10–14). III. He praises the Lord for this deliverance (15–18). The third part (C) is a kind of colloquy between the psalmist, the priests, and the people (19–29). I. It begins as they are about to enter the temple (19–25). II. It continues in the temple itself (26–29).

1   *Alleluia.*

A   Give thanks to the Lord, for he is kind:
his mercy lasts eternally.
2   O let the house of Israel say:
"His mercy lasts eternally."
3   O let the house of Aaron say:
"His mercy lasts eternally."

⁴ Let all who fear the Lord exclaim:
"His mercy lasts eternally."

I   ⁵ Deep in my trouble I invoked the Lord;
the Lord heard me and rescued me.

⁶ The Lord is with me; no fear have I;
what can man do to me?

⁷ The Lord, my helper, is with me,
and I shall see my foes discomfited.

⁸ 'Tis better far to fly to the Lord for help,
than trust in man.

⁹ 'Tis better far to fly to the Lord for help,
than trust in men of rank and power.

II ¹⁰ The nations all had compassed me:
in the Lord's name I ground them down.

¹¹ They compassed me on every side:
in the Lord's name I ground them down.

¹² They swarmed 'round me like bees;
they burnt me, just as fire burns thorns:
in the Lord's name I ground them down.

¹³ Pushed and shoved I was, that I might fall;
but the Lord has been my help.

¹⁴ My strength and courage is the Lord;
a savior he has proved himself to me.

III ¹⁵ A cry of jubilee and of deliverance
went up in the tents of the saints:
the Lord's right hand did valiantly;

¹⁶ the Lord's right hand uplifted me;
the Lord's right hand did valiantly.

¹⁷ I shall not die; no, I shall live,
and publish all the Lord has done.

117:5–18. The speaker in these lines seems to be uttering the thoughts of the people in general.

117B:9b. *men of rank and power*: by much experience, Israel had learned that princes and kings could be of no help.

117B:10–12. The description of the peril and the battle is metaphorical and hyperbolical.

117B:15b. *tents of the saints*: this probably means the tents in which the Israelites were accustomed to dwell during the festival days of autumn.

18 The Lord chastised me grievously!
But oh, to death he did not hand me over.

C I **19** Open to me the holy gates;
I will go in through them and thank the Lord.
20 This is the Lord's own gate:
the holy shall go in by it.
21 I will give thanks to you for hearing me;
a savior you have proved yourself to me.
22 The stone the builders have rejected —
it has become the cornerstone.
23 This is the doing of the Lord:
a wondrous thing for us to see.
24 This is the day the Lord has made:
let us exult in rapturous joy.
25 Grant safety, Lord;
Lord, grant prosperity!

II **26** Blest is the man who comes in the name of the Lord.
We bless you — from the house of the Lord.
27 The Lord is God! His kindly glance appeared to us!
Arrange the solemn march! Strew leafy boughs
as far as the horns of the altar!
28 My God you are! I give you thanks!
My God, I praise you to the skies!
29 Give thanks to the Lord, for he is kind;
his mercy lasts eternally.

117B:19, 20. The solemn procession arrives at the gates of the temple
and the marchers ask to be admitted (cf. Pss. 14 and 23).

117C:22b. *the cornerstone*: the people of Israel, rejected and trodden down
by mighty kingdoms, was chosen by God to be the cornerstone of the
messianic kingdom. Using these words in a more perfect sense, Christ applied
them to himself (cf. Mt. 21:42–44).

117C:26. The priests bless those coming into the temple.

117C:27c. *horns of the altar*: i.e., the altar of holocausts, which stood in
the court of the priests in the temple; its four corners projected like horns.

PSALM 118

Praise of the Law

This, the longest of the psalms, pays tribute to the excellence of the divine law, i.e., supernatural revelation, as the norm of life.

The psalm is alphabetical (cf. Introduction, Ps. 9). Hence, there is no strict logical connection in the thoughts presented; in the individual strophes, however, one general thought, for the most part, prevails.

Aleph

Blessed are they who observe God's law.

1 O well for those whose ways are innocent,
   who walk the ways the law of the Lord enjoins.
2 O well for those who carry out what he prescribes,
   and go wholeheartedly in quest of him;
3 who do no wrong,
   but walk his ways.
4 You gave your precepts
   to be obeyed with care.
5 Would that my steps were firm
   and thus complied with your demands!
6 I shall not then be shamed
   when I attend to all that you command.
7 My praise of you will be sincere
   when I have learnt your just decrees.
8 O let me cherish your behests,
   and do not utterly abandon me.

Beth

Gladly will I observe your law.

9 How will a youth preserve his innocence?
   By cherishing your words.
10 With my whole heart I am in quest of you:
    O do not let me swerve from your commands.
11 Deep in my heart I shrine your utterance:
    O may I give you no offence.

12 Blest are you, Lord;
   O teach me your behests.
13 My lips tell out the tale
   of the decrees your lips have passed.
14 The ways you have prescribed — they are my joy;
   like they are to all amassèd wealth.
15 Upon your precepts will I meditate,
   and study out your ways.
16 Your laws shall be my pleasure,
   and I shall not forget your words.

Ghimel

Give me the grace to follow your law, even in the midst of persecutions.

17 Befriend your servant: I wish to live
   and cherish all your words.
18 Open my eyes:
   I wish to scan the wonders of your law.
19 A pilgrim am I here on earth:
   do not conceal from me what you demand.
20 My soul consumes itself —
   so constantly I yearn for your decrees!
21 You have rebuked the proud;
   cursed are those who deviate from your commands.
22 Save me from opprobrium and contempt;
   for, all your precepts I observe.
23 Let mighty men, together leagued, speak to my detriment:
   your servant ponders on your laws.
24 Indeed, your precepts are my soul's delight;
   your laws — they are my counselors!

Daleth

When I am plagued with trouble, I beseech you to teach and console me.

118:19. Since I am only a pilgrim here, it is proper that I make good use of this brief space of time.

118:24b. *my counselors:* he does not follow the counsels of great men who contemn the law of God.

25 My soul lies prostrate in the dust:
 give life to me again according to your word.
26 I bared my ways: you answered me;
 teach me what you would have me do.
27 Instruct me in the ways your law commands,
 and on your wonders will I meditate.
28 My soul sheds tears from grief:
 cheer me according to your word.
29 Preserve me from the devious way;
 grant that I faithfully observe your law.
30 The true, straight path — that is my choice;
 your precepts are my guiding star.
31 I cling to your commands;
 O Lord, do not discomfit me.
32 The way of your commandments will I run
 once you expand my heart with joy.

He

Give me light and grace to follow your law faithfully.

33 Show me, O Lord, what your decrees demand;
 and I will keep them perfectly.
34 O train me to observe your law,
 and I will cherish it with all my heart.
35 Guide me along the path your law enjoins;
 for that is my delight.
36 Incline my heart to welcome your demands,
 and not to welcome greed.
37 O turn my eyes from vanity,
 and give me life by holding to your way.
38 Redeem the promise to your servant made,
 the promise made to all your worshipers.
39 Avert the shame of which I am afraid:
 your precepts soothe the heart.
40 You see, I am enamored of your law;
 then, in your fairness, give me life.

118:36, 37. *Greed:* i.e., the love of riches, and *vanity:* i.e., inane things, which both arouse concupiscence and greatly impede the observance of the law.

118:39. *shame:* sc., the derision and contempt of enemies; cf. v. 22.

Vau

I will make profession of your law before the great ones of this earth.

41 Lord, may your mercies come to me;
   your help, for you have promised it.
42 Then shall I answer those who censure me;
   for in your words I put my trust.
43 Let me forever be in words and deeds sincere;
   in your decrees I put my trust.
44 I will at all times keep your law,
   forever and eternally.
45 And I shall walk a wide and spacious path,
   because I search out your commands.
46 And of your precepts will I speak when face to face with royalty,
   and I shall never be discomfited.
47 In your commandments will I take delight;
   I love them from my heart.
48 With hand and heart I greet your laws,
   and meditate on your decrees.

Zain

In affliction and sorrow your law is my solace and joy.

49 Recall your promise to your servant made,
   by which you gave me hope.
50 This is my solace when I come to grief:
   your word gives me another lease of life.
51 The proud insult me grossly;
   but from your law I do not deviate.
52 Lord, I recall your judgments made of old;
   this it is that comforts me.
53 How indignation seizes me
   because the sinners set aside your law!
54 Your laws are themes of song to me
   while I am on my pilgrimage.
55 Mindful of your name at night am I,
   and I will keep your law.
56 This privilege has been bestowed on me,
   because your precepts I have kept.

Heth

My firm resolution is to observe your law; to sinners I am opposed; to your worshipers I am a friend.

⁵⁷ And I declare: the part assigned to me, O Lord,
is to comply with your commands.
⁵⁸ With all my heart I ask your kindly look:
have mercy on me as you have promised me.
⁵⁹ I pondered on my ways,
and I direct my steps toward keeping your decrees.
⁶⁰ I have been eager, and did not delay,
to cherish your commands.
⁶¹ The ropes of sinners coiled me round;
but I did not forget your law.
⁶² At dead of night I rise to give you thanks
for all your just decrees.
⁶³ I am a friend of all your worshipers,
of those who cherish your commands.
⁶⁴ Your kindness overflows the earth, O Lord;
teach me the rulings you have made.

Teth

Afflictions you sent me; they have taught me to observe your law.

⁶⁵ You acted kindly toward your worshiper,
O Lord, according to your word.
⁶⁶ O teach me judgment, teach me sense,
because in your commands I trust.
⁶⁷ I strayed, and then I came to grief;
but now I treasure up your utterance.
⁶⁸ How kind and how benevolent you are!
Teach me the rulings you have made.
⁶⁹ To do me harm, proud men resort to frauds:
but I, with all my heart, observe what you command.
⁷⁰ Gross are their minds — like fat;
but I take pleasure in your law.

118:70. *Gross . . . like fat:* their minds are heavy, sluggish; they do not feel the stimulus of the divine law (cf. Ps. 16:10).

71 How good it was for me to come to grief,
that I may learn what you ordain.
72 Better for me the law your lips proclaim —
better than heaps of silver and of gold.

Iod

**Tried with afflictions as I am, I ask you to console me and put my
enemies to shame.**

73 Your hands have made and fashioned me;
teach me to learn all your decrees.
74 Your worshipers are cheered at sight of me,
for in your word I firmly hope.
75 I know, your rulings, Lord, are just,
and justly you afflicted me.
76 Now let your mercy come to comfort me,
for to your servant you have pledged your word.
77 O may your mercies come to me, that I may live,
because your law is my delight.
78 Shame on the proud: they grieve me undeservedly;
upon your precepts I will ever meditate.
79 Let all who fear you follow me —
all those that take to heart your law.
80 My heart be perfect in observing your decrees,
that I may not be put to shame.

Caph

Oppressed by foes, I ardently desire and beseech your aid.

81 My soul is weary yearning for your aid;
and in your word I trust.
82 My eyes are weary yearning for your promised aid:
when will you comfort me?
83 Yes, I am like a wineskin in the smoke:
yet do I not forget what you ordain.
84 How many are the days your servant has to wait?
When will you judge the foes that pester me?

118:79. *follow me:* i.e., align themselves to me as friends and companions.
118:83. *a wineskin in the smoke:* in ancient oriental houses, wineskins
were hung from the ceiling and thus exposed to heat and smoke; as a result
they became dried out and wrinkled.

85 Proud men have pitfalls dug for me:
   they do not act according to your law.
86 Your rulings, one and all, are based on truth;
   help me; they persecute me undeservedly.
87 They threw me almost to the ground:
   yet I have not abandoned your decrees.
88 O, in your mercy, save my life;
   and I will keep the laws your lips proclaim.

Lamed

Your law is stable and pleasing; it knows no limits.

89 Your word, Lord, stands eternally,
   as firm as heaven itself.
90 From age to age endures your faithfulness,
   like the enduring earth which you have made.
91 They ever firmly stand by your decree;
   all things are serving you.
92 Were not your law my great delight,
   I should by now have perished in my grief.
93 Not in eternity shall I forget your hests,
   because by them you gave me life.
94 Yours I am: save me,
   because I make your precepts my concern.
95 Sinners lie in wait to ruin me;
   to your commandments I attend.
96 I see that every perfect thing is limited:
   all free from limitations is your law.

Mem

Your law is the source of wisdom and joy.

97 O how I love your law, O Lord!
   The livelong day I ponder it.
98 Your precepts make me wiser than my foes;
   I am forever wrapped in them.
99 More shrewd I am than all those teaching me,
   because I always ponder your decrees.

118:91. *They ever firmly stand:* sc., heaven (v. 89) and earth (v. 90).
118:96. What men call *perfect* always has some limitations. The divine law, however, knows no limitations.

100 I have more knowledge than old men,
     for I observe your laws.
101 I keep my feet from every evil way,
     that I may keep your laws.
102 From your decrees I do not deviate,
     because you have instructed me.
103 How sweet to my palate are your words —
     more sweet than honey to my mouth!
104 Your precepts make me wise;
     hence I abhor whatever is iniquitous.

Nun

Your law is a light to me; even when afflicted and oppressed I shall observe it.

105 Your word — it is a lamp to guide my feet,
     a light to show my path.
106 I swear and I resolve
     to carry out your just demands.
107 My suffering is keen, O Lord;
     keep me alive according to your word.
108 Accept, O Lord, the offerings I make;
     and teach me your decrees.
109 Imperilled is my life at every step;
     yet do I not forget your law.
110 A snare have sinners laid for me;
     yet from your precepts I have not diverged.
111 Your precepts are my everlasting heritage,
     because they are my heart's delight.
112 I have inclined my heart to carry out what you command,
     eternally, most perfectly.

Samech

Those whom you abominate, I, too, detest.

113 All men of double mind I loathe;
     I love your law.

118:103. *sweet to my palate:* cf. Ps. 18:11.
118:108. He offers his promises and prayers as sacrifices are offered.
118:113. *double mind:* those who waver between fidelity to God and defection from him.

114 My shelter and my shield are you:
and in your word I trust.
115 Depart from me, all evil-minded men;
I will observe all that my God commands.
116 According to your promise, bear me up: and I shall live.
O do not thwart my hope!
117 Help me, and then I shall be safe,
and I will always heed what you command.
118 You spurn all those that stray from your behests:
their thought is based upon a lie.
119 As dross you count all sinners in the world;
therefore I love all your decrees.
120 For fear of you, I shudder, body and soul;
all your decrees I treat with reverence.

Ain

Since I love your law, delay not in giving me aid against proud men.

121 Right and justice are my norm of action;
to my oppressors do not give me up.
122 Be surety for your servant's happiness,
or else the proud will trample me.
123 My eyes are weary longing for your help,
and for the holy promise you have made.
124 According to your kindness treat your worshiper;
and teach me all you have decreed.
125 I am your servant; teach me, then,
that I may know what you would have me do.
126 Time for the Lord it is to act;
they violate your law.
127 Therefore I cherish your commandments
more than the purest gold.
128 Therefore your rulings are my rule;
and every form of falsehood I abhor.

118:119. *dross:* i.e., things which are cast aside as of no value.
118:122. *Be surety for your servant's happiness:* when my own strength
fails me, do you act in my place.

Phe

Instruct and protect the admirer and lover of your law.

¹²⁹ Full of wonder are your precepts;
I therefore keep them faithfully.
¹³⁰ The unfolding of your words gives light,
instructs the inexperienced;
¹³¹ and I, with open mouth, inhale the air;
so ardently I long for your commands.
¹³² O turn to me and pity me, as you are wont
to do toward all who love your name.
¹³³ Direct my steps by your decrees;
may malice never master me.
¹³⁴ Deliver me from men that harass me,
and I will cherish your commands.
¹³⁵ A kindly look grant to your worshiper,
and teach me your decrees.
¹³⁶ Rills of water from my eyes have flowed,
because men did not keep your laws.

Sade

Just, firm, pure is your law.

¹³⁷ Just you are, O Lord;
your verdict, right.
¹³⁸ With justice you impose your laws,
and with great firmness.
¹³⁹ I am consumed with zeal,
because your foes forget your words!
¹⁴⁰ Your utterance has been tested and refined;
your servant is in love with it!
¹⁴¹ A little one I am; I am despised;
but your commands I never will forget.
¹⁴² Eternal is the justice of your law;
your law will never change.

118:131. *inhale the air:* so ardently do I long for your commands that I draw them in as I inhale the air.
118:135. Cf. Pss. 66:2; 79:4.
118:140. *tested and refined:* i.e., like metal, it has been purified as by fire and, therefore, is most pure (cf. Ps. 11:7).

143 Distress and tribulation have befallen me;
   your precepts are my great delight.
144 Eternal is the justice of your laws;
   teach me, and I shall live.

Coph

With all my heart do I ask that you give me the grace to keep your law.

145 I cry with all my heart: Lord, answer me:
   your statutes I observe.
146 I cry to you: save me;
   and I will cherish your behests.
147 I come at dawn, and I implore your help;
   my trust is in your words.
148 My eyes forestall the watches of the night,
   that I may meditate upon your utterance.
149 O hear my voice — you are so merciful!
   O give me life — for you have so decreed!
150 Those who unjustly harass me draw near;
   and to your law they pay no heed.
151 But near you are, O Lord;
   all your commands reveal your faithfulness.
152 Long have I known from your commands
   that you have founded them to last eternally.

Res

Save me from lying persecutors!

153 See my affliction: rescue me;
   for I do not forget your law.
154 Defend my cause; deliver me;
   as you have promised, grant me life.
155 For sinners, there is no redemption;
   they do not cherish your decrees.
156 Your kindnesses are numerous, O Lord;
   and as you have decided, grant me life.

118:148. *My eyes forestall the watches of the night:* i.e., I am awake before the hour of arising. Cf. v. 62; Ps. 76:5.

me,

157 Full many persecute and harass me;
   from your decrees I do not deviate.
158 I saw the faithless: it disgusted me;
   they do not heed your utterance.
159 Look, Lord; I cherish your decrees;
   and in your mercy save my life.
160 The chief distinction of your law is constancy;
   your just decisions stand eternally.

Sin

For me, your law is the source of reverence, peace, and joy.

161 Princes, unprovoked, are persecuting me;
   but from my heart I reverence your words.
162 I am delighted with your oracles,
   as when a man finds richest spoils.
163 All wickedness I hate and I detest;
   I love your law.
164 Seven times a day I speak your praise
   because of all your just decrees.
165 Deep peace alights on those who love your law;
   for them there is no stumbling block.
166 I look for your deliverance, O Lord;
   I carry out all your behests.
167 I cherish your commands with all my heart;
   I am in love with them exceedingly.
168 I cherish your commands and your decrees;
   for in your sight I live my daily life.

Tau

Let my prayer arise to you; deliver me, lead me, for without you I am a straying sheep.

169 O may my cry reach out to you, O Lord;
   according to your promise lesson me.
170 O may my pleading reach your throne;
   according to your promise rescue me.

118:164. *Seven times a day:* i.e., often (cf. Ps. 11:7).

171 And may my lips pour forth a hymn of praise,
since you have taught me your decrees.
172 O may my tongue extol your oracle,
because all your demands are just.
173 O may your hand be ready, helping me,
for, your decrees — they are my choice!
174 I crave salvation at your hands, O Lord;
your law is my delight.
175 O may I live and give you praise;
and may your precepts be a help to me.
176 I wander like a straying sheep: come, seek your worshiper,
for your commands I never will forget.

PSALM 119

A Protest Against Wicked Tongues

I. The psalmist, dwelling among men whose words cannot be trusted, asks God that he may be kept free from their deceits (1, 2). II. These men, he says, will receive severe punishments (3, 4). III. He regrets that he must live among them for so long a time (5–7).

Psalms 119 to 133 were called "Songs of Ascents" or "Songs for the Goings-Up." They were most probably given this title because they were sung by the Israelites as they went up to the temple, three times in the year, for their great feasts (cf. Exod. 23:17; Deut. 16:16).

1 A Song of Ascents.

I   To the Lord I cried in my distress,
and he has heard my prayer.
2 O Lord, save me again from wicked lips,
again from guileful tongues!

II   3 What punishment condign have you deserved,
O guileful tongue?
4 Sharp-pointed arrows from a brawny arm,
the broom plant's glowing coals!

119:3, 4. The *punishment condign* will be *sharp-pointed arrows*, i.e., certain death, and the *broom plant's glowing coals*, i.e., intensely hot fire. The wood of the broom plant was very hard; when burnt, it produced an extremely hot charcoal that glowed for a long time.

III   ⁵ Alas, alas! In Mosoch is my home,
        I dwell in Cedar's tents!
      ⁶ Too long have I been living
        with men, the mortal enemies of peace!
      ⁷ I plead for peace;
        they press for war!

PSALM 120

God, the Preserver and Protector of His Temple

I. The psalmist states that his help comes from God (1, 2). II. Faithfully and constantly, he watches over his people (3, 4). III. He protects them night and day (5, 6). IV. Always and in all places, he defends them from all harm (7, 8).

      ¹ A song of Ascents.

I   Up to the mountains do I lift my eyes;
        O whence comes help to me?
      ² My help is from the Lord,
        the maker of heaven and earth.

II   ³ He will not suffer your foot to falter;
        your guardian will not sleep.
      ⁴ No, no; no sleeper and no slumberer he —
        the guardian of Israel!

III   ⁵ Your guardian is the Lord;
        to shelter you, the Lord stands on your right.
      ⁶ By day the sun will not strike you,
        nor will the moon by night.

119:5. *Mosoch:* a people living across the Euxine Sea; *Cedar's* has reference to a nomad tribe of the Syro-arabic desert. These two names are used metaphorically to signify barbarous and uncivilized people.

120:1. *the mountains:* namely, those in which was situated the Holy City and the Temple (cf. Pss. 86:1; 124:2).

120:6b. Even today Orientals believe that the moon can cause certain diseases. Another meaning may be that *moon* here stands for the cold and chill of the night.

V 7 The Lord will guard you from all harm;
     aye, he will guard your life.
   8 The Lord will guard your going out and coming in,
     both now and evermore.

PSALM 121

A Salute to Jerusalem, the Holy City

The psalmist stands at the gates of the city. I. He rejoices over his pilgrimage to Jerusalem and at the sight of the city which is so splendidly built (1–3). II. The Holy City is the people's chief place of worship of the true God and the seat of the high judges of his people (4, 5). III. The psalmist prays that the city will have peace and security (6–9).

1 *A song of Ascents.*

I   I am entranced because they said to me:
     "To the house of the Lord we go!"
   2 Already our feet are standing
     at your gates, Jerusalem —
   3 Jerusalem, built as a well-built city,
     compact, harmonious, in whole and part!

II 4 Here tribe on tribe of the Lord ascends
     to praise the name of the Lord as Israel's law demands.
   5 Here, too, the rulers' seats are placed,
     the seats of the rulers of David's house.

II 6 O pray for the peace of Jerusalem!
     May all that love you be secure!
   7 May there be peace within your walls,
     and safety in your stately homes!
   8 For the sake of my brethren and my friends
     I will say: "Peace be to you!"
   9 For the sake of the house of the Lord our God
     I will pray: "May all be well with you!"

Psalm 122

A Contemned People's Trust in God

I. The people compare themselves to a servant who depends entirely
on the beck and call of his master or mistress (1, 2). II. They ask
humbly that they might be liberated from the present state of
oppression and contempt (3, 4).

¹ A song of Ascents.

I   My eyes I lift to you
    who dwell in heaven above.
² Yes, as the eyes of servants
    turn to their masters' hands;
    as the eyes of a servant maid
    turn to her mistress' hands:
    so turn our eyes to the Lord our God
    till he has mercy on us.

II ³ Have mercy on us, O Lord, have mercy on us;
    for we are glutted with contempt.
  ⁴ Our soul is glutted
    with rich men's taunts, with proud men's scorn.

Psalm 123

It Is the Lord Who Saves Us From Extreme Danger

I. The people, freed from a most harrowing danger, describe what
would have happened to them had not God come to their aid (1–5).
II. They render thanks for their delivery (6–8).

¹ A song of Ascents by David.

I   Had not the Lord been on our side —
    so Israel may now say —
² had not the Lord been on our side,
    when men assaulted us,
³ they would have swallowed us alive.
    And when their fury flared at us,

4 then would the flood have buried us;
 then would a torrent have swept o'er us;
5 then would a swollen stream have swept us off.

II 6 Blest be the Lord, who did not give us up —
 a victim to their crunching teeth!
 7 Our lives were rescued like a bird
 from fowler's snare.
 Demolished is the snare,
 and we are freed!
 8 Our help is in the name of the Lord,
 the maker of heaven and earth!

PSALM 124

God Is the Helper of His People Against
Their Enemies

**I. The Lord surrounds his people with his protection as the moun-
tains hedge in the city of Jerusalem (1, 2). II. Thus protected, the
faithful will not be conquered by the wicked (3). III. May God,
therefore, quickly give his help (4, 5).**

1 A song of Ascents.

I Those who trust in the Lord are like Mount Sion:
 it does not move; it stands eternally!
 2 Mountains surround Jerusalem:
 just so the Lord surrounds his chosen race
 both now and evermore.

II 3 The sinners' sway shall not remain
 upon the lot of saints;
 and thus the saints will not reach out
 their hands to perpetrate iniquity.

123:4–6. In two metaphors, namely, that of a raging torrent, which sweeps
everything before it, and a voracious beast, which devours its victims, the
psalmist depicts the danger and helplessness of his people.
124:3c. *the saints will not reach out*, etc.: persecution by the wicked
readily leads to the fall of those whose faith is weak.

III ⁴ Befriend, O Lord, the good
     and true of heart.
   ⁵ But those who stray into their crooked paths,
     may the Lord expel them with the wicked crowd!
     Peace hover over Israel!

PSALM 125

A Prayer for the Total Restoration of the People

**I. The people rejoice over their liberation from the Babylonian Exile
(1–3). II. Since, however, the troubles they now suffer show that
total restoration (i.e., the messianic one) has not yet been given
them, they petition the Lord that, when the lot of the people has
been changed, these unhappy conditions of things will be followed
by a joyful and abundant harvest (4–6).**

¹ A song of Ascents.

I   When the Lord brought Sion's captive children back,
      it seemed all like a dream to us!
   ² Our faces then were wreathed in smiles;
     our tongues were jubilant with joy.
     Then said the Gentiles 'mongst themselves:
     "The Lord has wondrously dealt with them!"
   ³ The Lord did wondrously deal with us!
     With joy we were transported!

II   ⁴ O change our lot, O Lord —
      as torrents oft the Southland do!
    ⁵ The men who sow in tears
      are wont to reap in bliss:
    ⁶ they go and go, and weep,
      as they carry the seed to be sown;
      they come and come, in bliss,
      as they carry their sheaves with them!

124:5. Let the lot of the Israelites who are unfaithful be the same as that
of the enemies who oppress the Chosen People.

125:4b. *torrents oft the Southland:* the Southland (the desert of Negeb),
dry and parched in summer, is changed into green and blooming fields when,
in late autumn, the watercourses are flooded with the fall rains.

PSALM 126

All Prosperity Is a Blessing of God

I. The labors of a man without the aid of God are vain (1, 2).
II. Children are a blessing of God; so, too, is the prosperity that a family enjoys (3–5).

¹ A song of Ascents by Solomon.

I   Unless the Lord erects the house,
in vain is the toil of the builders;
unless the Lord protects the city,
in vain is the watch of the guards.
² In vain it is for you to rise before the dawn,
to sit up late into the night —
for you who eat the hard-earned bread.
In sleep he gives plenty to those whom he loves.

II ³ Children, too, are the gift of the Lord;
the fruit of the womb is a reward!
⁴ What arrows are in a warrior's hand,
that are the children begotten in youth.
⁵ Happy the man who fills his quiver with these:
they shall not blush when they vie with their foes at the city gate.

PSALM 127

Domestic Happiness of a Good Israelite

I. The psalmist hails the happiness of him who reverences the Lord: he will be blessed in his labors, his wife, and his children (1–4).
II. May such a man, the psalmist prays, enjoy a long life in the prosperous city of Jerusalem (5, 6).

126:4b. The children will help and sustain the father when he grows old.
126:5. The figure of the preceding verse is resumed.
126:5b. The courts were held at the city gates; in these the sons will defend a father who is unjustly accused.

¹ A song of Ascents.

I   O well for you who fear the Lord
and walk the ways he has enjoined!
² For you shall eat the earnings of your own hands;
you shall be blest; it shall be well with you.
³ Your wife shall be as a fruitful vine
within the chambers of your home.
Your children shall be like to olive shoots
ranged round your board.
⁴ Thus, mark, shall he be blessed —
the man who fears the Lord.

II ⁵ The Lord bless you from Sion Mount
that you may see Jerusalem's prosperity in all the days of your life;
⁶ that you may see your children's children!
May peace be over Israel!

Psalm 128

Israel, Assailed From Its Youth, Implores the Aid of God

I. The psalmist recalls what his people suffered in earlier days: they were constantly being tried, but they were never overcome (1–4). II. This memory makes him confident; he asks that now again the enemy may be repulsed (5–8).

¹ A song of Ascents.

I   They have assailed me fiercely from my youth,
so may now Israel say;
² they have assailed me fiercely from my youth;
but they have not defeated me!

127:2. *you shall eat the earnings*: i.e., the things that you have prepared by your own hands you shall enjoy, and no calamity or evil will take them from you. For this reason, *it shall be well with you.*

127:5, 6. To the blessing mentioned in the preceding verses, the psalmist adds two more: tranquil days in the prosperous and peaceful city of Jerusalem and a long life. The psalmist here promises earthly blessings, in keeping with the general character of the Old Testament.

³ Upon my back the plowmen plowed;
   they drew their furrows long!
⁴ But then the Lord was just:
   he cut the bonds of wicked men.

II   ⁵ Let them be shamed and driven back —
      all Sion's enemies!
   ⁶ Let them become like grass upon the roof,
      which fades ere it is plucked.
   ⁷ No reaper fills his hand with it,
      no gleaner of sheaves his arms.
   ⁸ Nor do the passers-by exclaim:
      "A blessing of the Lord on you!"
      "We bless you in the name of the Lord!"

PSALM 129

Man's Sins; God's Mercy

I. The psalmist, from the depths of his sins, calls upon God (1, 2).
II. We are all sinners; only God's pardon can save us (3, 4).
III. With trust and yearning, let the sinner look for this indulgence
(5–6b). IV. May the people of Israel cherish this same hope of
pardon and, ultimately, of full redemption (6c–8).
   This is the sixth of the penitential psalms. It is also used in
liturgical prayers for the dead.

¹ A song of Ascents.

I   Out of the depths I cry to you, O Lord;
   ² Lord, hear my voice!
      O be your ears attentive
      to the voice of my entreating!

II   ³ Should you keep record of transgressions, Lord,
      then who, Lord, could endure?

128:6. The level roofs of the houses of ancient Palestine were covered
with mud. After rains, grass would sometimes take root and grow there.
When the sun arose, the grass withered, even before it could be pulled out.
So quickly, says the psalmist, may the enemies of Israel perish.
129:1. *Out of the depths:* i.e., the depths of his sins, not his troubles.

⁴ But in your gift is pardon of sins,
so that you may be served with reverence.

III ⁵ My trust is in the Lord;
my soul trusts in his word.
⁶ My soul awaits the Lord
more eagerly than watchman waits for dawn.

IV   More eagerly than watchman waits for dawn
⁷ may Israel await the Lord.
For in the gift of the Lord is mercy,
and in his gift is plentiful ransom;
⁸ and he will ransom Israel
from all its wickedness.

PSALM 130

With Childlike Simplicity,
the Psalmist Seeks Rest in God

The psalmist renounces pride of heart and the desire for things
beyond his powers. With composed and peaceful mind, he rests in
God, as an infant rests on the bosom of his mother.

¹ A song of Ascents by David.

O Lord, I am not proud of heart;
nor do my eyes roam haughtily.
I do not aim at lofty things,
at things too high for me!
² No, no; I ever keep my soul
composed, at perfect peace.
An infant in its mother's lap —
an infant — such my soul in me!
³ Trust, Israel, in the Lord,
both now and evermore.

129:4b. *so that you may be served with reverence:* the fruit of the pardon
obtained is a greater devotion and reverence toward God.

129:8. *he will ransom Israel:* i.e., on the day of messianic salvation, as
the prophets had promised.

PSALM 131

David's Promises to God; God's Promises to David

The psalm has two parts. (A: 1–10). I. David promises, under oath, that he will build a fitting abode for the Ark in Jerusalem (1–5). II. These promises will be fulfilled when the Ark has been enshrined in the temple (6–10). (B: 11–18). I. With solemn oath, God promises to King David the lasting continuance of his kingdom (11–13). II. The closing verses show how these promises are to be fulfilled (14–18).

¹ *A song of Ascents.*

A I   Be merciful to David, Lord;
remember all his anxious care:
  ² how he made oath to the Lord,
and made a vow to Jacob's Mighty One:
  ³ "I will not enter my beloved home,
or climb into the couch prepared for me;
  ⁴ I will allow my eyes no sleep,
or grant my eyelids rest —
  ⁵ till I have found a place for the Lord,
a dwelling place for Jacob's Mighty One."

II ⁶ Mark well: we heard of it in Ephrata,
we found it in the Iaar plains.
  ⁷ O let us enter, then, his dwelling place,
fall down before the footstool of his feet.
  ⁸ Rise, Lord! On to your resting place,
you, and the Ark that shrines your majesty!

131:6. They heard of the Ark (it is mentioned in v. 7), which was to be taken to Jerusalem, in Ephrata, i.e., Bethlehem, the city of David; then they found it *in the Iaar plains*, i.e., Cariathiarim, where it had long been. Cariathiarim was in the district of Ephrata. On this location of the Ark, see 1 Sam. 7:1, 2; 2 Sam. 6:2; 1 Par. 13:1–8.

131:7b. *the footstool of his feet:* when the Lord was present over the Ark (cf. Pss. 79:2; 98:1), it was called the footstool of his feet.

131:8. After the Ark had been moved from Silo, it had no fixed repository. Hence, the reference here to its final resting place.

⁹ O bid your priests to don the robe of holiness,
and may your servants leap with joy!
¹⁰ To please your servant David,
do not disdain the face of your anointed one.

B I ¹¹ A solemn pledge the Lord to David gave —
sworn to — nor will he e'er be false to it:
"An offspring of your line
will I set on your throne.
¹² If your descendants keep my pact,
obey what precepts I shall give to them,
their children also shall forever sit
upon your throne."
¹³ The Lord, you see, has chosen Sion
and wishes it to be his seat.

II ¹⁴ "Here is my resting place forevermore;
here will I dwell, for I have chosen it.
¹⁵ Upon its food supply my blessing shall descend abundantly;
its poor shall have their fill of bread;
¹⁶ its priests will I invest with holy gifts;
its saints shall be in transports of delight.
¹⁷ There will I raise up David's mighty line,
for my anointed one prepare a lamp.
¹⁸ His foes will I wrap round with shame;
upon his head shall shine my diadem."

Psalm 132

Joy of Fraternal Harmony

The psalmist uses two images that were familiar to the Orientals
to depict how admirable is harmony among brothers. The first is
that of the sacred oil of unction; it flows smoothly from the head to
the beard and then to the very edge of the garment; the second

---

131:10b. anointed one: this is not only David, but also his successors.
The people ask for a blessing on the successive kings for David's sake.

131:11, 12. Cf. 2 Sam. 7:8–16; Ps. 88:4–5, 29–38.

131:17b. lamp: used symbolically to indicate descendants, posterity. anointed
one: here, David himself.

131:18. These verses refer to the Messias.

is that of the dew which falls abundantly on Mount Sion in the morning. Like to these are the blessings wherewith God rewards fraternal harmony.

1 A *song of Ascents.*

O mark how pleasant and how good it is
when brethren dwell in perfect unison!
2 It is like finest oil poured on the head —
down on the beard it flows, on Aaron's beard,
and down it flows to his vestment's edge!
3 Or like to Hermon dew,
the dew distilled on Sion's hill!
'Tis here the Lord his benediction lavishes —
aye, life to last forevermore.

Psalm 133

Evensong in the Temple

This short chant seems to have been used in the Temple at the close of the day, when one group of levites were leaving after their service in the Temple and another group were coming in to replace them. Those departing exhort those who are arriving to praise God throughout the night (1, 2). These latter, or one of them, bless the departing ones (3).

1 A *song of Ascents.*

Come, bless the Lord,
all you who serve the Lord,
who stay in the house of the Lord
at nightly hours.
2 Uplift your hands to the sanctuary,
and bless the Lord.

3 May you be blessed from Sion by the Lord,
the maker of heaven and earth.

132:2. In the consecration of the high priest, oil was poured upon his head.
132:3. *Hermon dew:* the dew on Mount Hermon was taken as typical of an exceptionally heavy dewfall.
132:3c. *'Tis here:* i.e., where brethren dwell in harmony.
133:1b. Those *who serve the Lord* are the priests and levites (cf. Deut. 10:8).

Psalm 134

Praise of God, Lord of All Things and Benefactor of His People Israel

At the beginning (A: 1–4) and at the end of this psalm (C: 19–21), the Israelites are called upon to praise God. In the middle section (B: 5–18) reasons are assigned why the Israelites should honor God. I. He is the Lord of nature (5–7). II. His aid to his people is powerful and generous (8–14). III. The idols of the heathens have no power (15–18).

1 *Alleluia.*

A   O praise the name of the Lord;
       give praise, O servants of the Lord,
2 all you who stay in the house of the Lord,
       within the courts of the house of our God.
3 O praise the Lord, because the Lord is kind;
       and hymn his name, for it is sweet.
4 The Lord has chosen Jacob for himself,
       and Israel for his property.

B I 5 For one, I know this much: great is the Lord;
       our ruler is above all gods.
6 The Lord accomplishes whate'er he will, in heaven and on earth,
       upon the sea, yes, in its deepest depth.
7 He brings on clouds from the end of the earth;
       his lightnings make the rain to fall;
       and from its caves he brings the wind.

  II 8 He slew the first-born things of Egypt,
       both man and beast alike;
9 he wrought stupendous portents, Egypt, in your midst,
       to frustrate Pharaoh and all his servile bands;
10 he vanquished many heathen tribes,
       and slaughtered mighty kings:

134:5. A priest is introduced as speaking here.
134:5b. gods: i.e., those who are called gods (cf. Ps. 96:9), but are in reality only idols fashioned by human hands (vv. 15–18).
134:7. Between the lightning flashes and peals of thunder, rain pours down.

11 Sehon, Amoria's king, and Og, the king of Basan,
and all the kings of Chanaan.
12 He gave their land, to have and hold eternally,
to Israel, his chosen race.
13 O Lord, your name eternally endures;
O Lord, your memory is green from age to age.
14 The Lord protects his chosen race,
and to his servants he is merciful.

III 15 The heathen idols are but silver and gold,
the work of human hands.
16 They have a mouth, but do not speak;
and they have eyes, but do not see;
17 and they have ears, but do not hear;
and in their mouths there is no breath.
18 Like them are all that fashion them,
and everyone that trusts in them.

C 19 O house of Israel, bless the Lord;
O house of Aaron, bless the Lord;
20 O house of Levi, bless the Lord;
O worshipers of the Lord, bless the Lord.
21 Blest be the Lord from Sion's hill,
the Lord who dwells within Jerusalem.

PSALM 135

Thanksgiving for the Manifold Blessings of God

In the proem, all faithful people are called upon to praise God (1–3). Some of his many blessings are enumerated. I. He created and fashioned the world (4–9). II. He protected, defended, and directed his people (10–22). III. His care over all men is ceaseless (23–26).

This psalm is written in the manner of a litany; after each title given to God, the refrain, "for his mercy lasts forever," is introduced.

1 *Alleluia.*

Praise the Lord, for he is kind,
for his mercy lasts forever.

134:15–18. Cf. Ps. 113:4–8.
134:19–20. Cf. Ps. 117:1–4.

² Praise the God of gods,
for his mercy lasts forever.
³ Praise the Lord of lords,
for his mercy lasts forever.

I   ⁴ Who alone did wondrous things,
for his mercy lasts forever.
⁵ Who with wisdom made the heavens,
for his mercy lasts forever.
⁶ Who spread the earth above the waters,
for his mercy lasts forever.
⁷ Who fashioned mighty luminaries,
for his mercy lasts forever;
⁸ the sun to rule the day,
for his mercy lasts forever;
⁹ the moon and stars to rule the night,
for his mercy lasts forever.

II ¹⁰ Who smote the Egyptians in their first-born,
for his mercy lasts forever.
¹¹ And led forth Israel from their midst,
for his mercy lasts forever.
¹² With mighty hand and extended arm,
for his mercy lasts forever.
¹³ Who parted the Red Sea,
for his mercy lasts forever.
¹⁴ And through its midst led Israel,
for his mercy lasts forever.
¹⁵ And plunged Pharaoh and his host into the Red Sea,
for his mercy lasts forever.
¹⁶ Who led his people through the wilderness,
for his mercy lasts forever.
¹⁷ Who struck down lofty kings,
for his mercy lasts forever.
¹⁸ Who slaughtered mighty kings,
for his mercy lasts forever:
¹⁹ Sehon, Amoria's king,
for his mercy lasts forever,
²⁰ and Og, king of Basan,
for his mercy lasts forever;

²¹ and gave their land into the possession,
for his mercy lasts forever,
²² into the possession of Israel, his servant,
for his mercy lasts forever.

III ²³ Who when we were abject remembered us,
for his mercy lasts forever.
²⁴ And from our foes he rescued us,
for his mercy lasts forever.
²⁵ Who gives food to every living thing,
for his mercy lasts forever.
²⁶ Give praise to heaven's God,
for his mercy lasts forever.

PSALM 136

Grief and Longings of the Exiles

The psalmist has returned to his fatherland from exile. I. He recalls how the Babylonian oppressors had demanded that the sorrowing exiles should sing for them their sacred songs of Sion (1–3). II. The exiles, faithful to their Holy City of Jerusalem, indignantly refused to do this (4–6). III. The psalmist prays that dire ruin may come to the Edomites and Babylonians because of their inhumanity (7–9).

I ¹ By Babylon's great waters, there we sat and wept
as we remembered Sion's Hill.
² Upon the willows of that land
we hung our harps;
³ for there our capturers asked songs of us;
and our tormentors asked for mirth:
"Sing some of Sion's songs for us!"

II ⁴ How can we sing the Lord's own song
on an alien soil?

136:1. *great waters:* the Euphrates and the Tigris and the extensive system of irrigating canals, which the Babylonians also called rivers.
136:2b. *we hung our harps:* because of grief, they could not play their instruments.
136:3. They asked for songs either out of curiosity or in derision.

⁵ If I forget you, O Jerusalem,
may my right hand forget its skill!
⁶ And may my tongue cleave to my jaws,
if I do not remember you,
and do not make Jerusalem
the summit of my joy!

III ⁷ Remember, Lord, despite the Edomites,
Jerusalem's woeful day,
and how they said: "Destroy her,
root and branch! Destroy!"
⁸ Men of the devastatrix Babylon —
blessed is he who will repay to you
the evils you have brought on us!
⁹ Blessed is he who snatches up your little ones
and dashes them against a rock!

PSALM 137

Thanksgiving for a Blessing

I. The psalmist gives thanks for a blessing received (1–3). II. He desires that all the kings of earth praise the Lord (4–6). III. With all trust, he prays that God will bless the good work that he has already begun (7, 8).

¹ A psalm of David.

I   I praise you, Lord, with my whole heart,
because you heard my pleading words.
I join the angels making melody to you,
² and prostrate fall within your holy shrine.
I sing the praises of your name,
because faithful you are and kind;

136:5, 6. The violence of speech here shows how offensive the demand was to the exiles.

136:7–9. Jerusalem was not only the fatherland of the exiles, but the Holy City, the seat of God. Hence they felt that a crime committed against it was a crime against God and, as such, it demanded fit punishment. The psalmist is speaking according to the law of retribution (the *lex talionis*) which obtained in the ancient Orient (cf. Introduction, Ps. 108).

because you have exalted o'er all else
your promise and your name.

3 You answered me what time I called on you,
and ample strength you put into my soul.

II   4 And all earth's kings will praise you, Lord,
on hearing of the promises you made;

5 and they will praise the ways of the Lord:
"In truth, great is the glory of the Lord!"

6 In truth, transcendent is the Lord: he looks with favor on the
humble man,
but on the proud he from a distance keeps an eye!

III   7 I wade a sea of trouble: you keep me still alive!
To screen me from my enemies' wrath, you reach your hand!
Your right hand keeps me safe!

8 In my behalf the Lord will finish what he has begun.
O Lord, your kindness lasts eternally.
Leave not undone the work of your own hands.

PSALM 138

God Is Present Everywhere, Sees All Things

I. The psalmist marvels at God's intimate knowledge of him (1–6).
II. The power and presence of God are universal (7–12). III. God,
the psalmist says, formed his body and his soul, foresaw the actions
of his life, set a limit to his days; the designs of God are beyond his
understanding (13–18). IV. At the close of the psalm, he expresses
his hatred for wicked men (19–24).

1 *To the choirmaster. A psalm of David.*

I   You search me and you know me, Lord:

2 you know me when I sit or rise;
you understand my thoughts from afar;

3 do I walk or do I lie down — you know me thoroughly,
on all my ways you keep an eye.

4 A word is not yet on my tongue;
already, you know it all!

5 Behind and in the front you compass me,
and hold your hand poised over me.

⁶ To me this knowledge is a passing wonder;
 it is sublime, beyond my grasp!

II ⁷ Where can I go to escape your Spirit?
 And whither can I fly to flee your face?
 ⁸ If I should mount to heaven, you are there;
 if in the realm of death I spread my couch, there, too, you are;
 ⁹ were I to take the wings of dawn,
 or dwell upon the outmost border of the sea,
 ¹⁰ there, too, your hand will be my guide,
 your right palm my support.
 ¹¹ Were I to say: "The dark, at least, will wrap me round,
 and night, instead of light, will compass me,"
 ¹² the very dark will not be dark to you:
 the night will be like to the glaring day:
 the same to you are dark and light.

III ¹³ Indeed, my inmost being you have formed,
 within my mother's womb you wove my texture.
 ¹⁴ I praise you — so marvellously am I made,
 so wondrous are your works.
 My soul you know most perfectly;
 ¹⁵ and nothing in my being is concealed from you.
 When I was formed in secrecy,
 and woven in the earth's deepest deep,
 ¹⁶ your eyes saw my development,
 and all my steps were written in your book.
 Days were decreed before there was but one of them.
 ¹⁷ For me, how hard to grasp are your designs, O God;
 and how immense their sum!
 ¹⁸ If I would count them o'er, more than the sand they are;
 were I to reach the end of them, you still are there for me to grasp!

IV ¹⁹ O would you slew the wicked one, O God;
 and that bloodthirsty men withdrew from me!

138:19–22. It is difficult to see the connection between these verses and
the earlier part of the psalm. Perhaps the psalmist wishes to express to God,
who scrutinizes all things, his own sincere and complete hatred for wicked
men (cf. v. 22). Or he may mean that he marvels that God, who knows
all things, permits the wicked to continue in life, or, again, that men can be
so wicked as to rise up against the all-high God.

20 With malice they revolt from you;
your foes behave most treacherously.
21 Do I not hate all those who hatred have for you, O Lord?
And are not your assailants my disgust?
22 I hate them with a perfect hate;
they have become my enemies!
23 Seach me, O God, and know my heart;
try me, and know my sentiments.
24 See if my way of life is crooked,
and lead me in the way of olden times.

Psalm 139

Against Violent and Base Enemies

I. The psalmist asks God to liberate him from violent and perfidious enemies (2–4). II. After he has described the deceits of such men, he implores God to help him (5–8). III. He prays that their plans may come to nought and that their evil may be turned back upon them (9–11). IV. Certain of the justice of God, he predicts for the enemies ruin; for good men, victory (12–14).

1 To the choirmaster. A psalm of David.

I 2 Rescue me, O Lord, from a wicked man;
screen me from a violent one —
3 from men whose hearts are set on wrong,
who stir up strife day after day.
4 Serpentlike, they edge their tongues;
the bane of asps lurks 'neath their lips.

II 5 Save me, Lord, from the clutch of a wicked man;
screen me from a violent one —
they plot to trip my feet.
6 Proud men lay hidden snares for me;
they spread out ropes to form a net,
and by the way place traps for me.

139:4. Cf. Pss. 54:22; 57:5.
139:6. As hunters set out snares and nets to catch animals, so the psalmist's enemies are scheming to trap him. Similar figures are used in Pss. 9:16; 30:5; 56:7; 63:6.

7 I say to the Lord: My God you are;
hear, Lord, my pleading voice.
8 Lord, God, my mighty help!
You shield my head in battle's day.

III   9 Lord, do not grant the wishes of the wicked man;
do not fulfill his plans.
10 Those who surround me carry high their heads.
O be the malice of their lips their grave.
11 May he rain burning coals on them,
and hurl them down into the pit to rise no more.

IV 12 The man of evil tongue does not live long on earth;
may ill luck swiftly overtake the violent man.
13 The Lord, I know so well, helps the needy to their right;
and to the poor sees justice done.
14 Assuredly, the good will celebrate your name;
the true of heart will dwell beneath your eyes.

PSALM 140

Prayer of a Just Man Against the Deceits of the Wicked

I. The psalmist asks that his prayer may ascend to God like the fumes of incense (1, 2). II. He begs God to preserve him from the ways of wicked men, for whom he predicts a fierce punishment (3–7). III. For himself, he asks salvation; for the foes, ruin (8–10).

1 A psalm of David.

I   O Lord, I cry to you: come promptly to my aid:
list to my voice whene'er I cry to you.
2 Like incense may my plea arise to you,
the lifting of my hands be an evening sacrifice.

II   3 Set, Lord, a guard beside my mouth,
and post a sentry at my lips.
4 Do not incline my heart to any evil thing,
to a career of heinous crime;
and may I never eat choice food
in company with wicked men.

5 Let some good man reprove me: it is a kindly act;
let him admonish me; like it is to oil poured on my head.
This will I not refuse to take;
no, I will always pray when humbled by good men.

6

7

III 8 To you, Lord God, are turned my eyes;
to you I confidently fly: O do not ruin me.
9 Protect me from the snare which they have laid for me,
and from the traps which wicked men have set.
10 Into the nets which they have set, let the wicked fall themselves,
while I escape unscathed.

PSALM 141

Cry of a Man Who Is Abandoned by All

I. In great distress the psalmist beseeches the help of God, who
knows well his present unhappy condition (2–4b). II. In this persecution he is destitute of all human aid (4c–5). III. He turns to God
and asks him to be his helper and deliverer; to God he will be
grateful (6–8).

1 A maskil of David, when he was in the cave. A prayer.

I   2 I loudly cry to the Lord;
and with the Lord I loudly plead.
3 I pour out in his presence all my care;
and in his presence bare all my anxiety.
4 Whene'er my spirit faints within me,
you know my way.

II   Along the way I tread
they laid a secret snare for me.

140:6 and 7 are left untranslated in Father Kleist's manuscript. The editors
of the Latin version state, in a footnote, that the original text of these verses
seems to be corrupt, and that their meaning is entirely obscure. Several in-
terpretations are suggested but the editors conclude that no one of them
is fully satisfactory.
141:4b. my way: i.e., my condition, my lot, both present and future.

5 I look to the right and see:
there is not one that cares for me.
And there is no escape for me;
and there is none concerned about my life.

III 6 I cry to you, O Lord;
I say: you are my safe retreat,
my portion in the land of life.
7 O listen to my cry;
I am a prey to utter wretchedness.
From my pursuers rescue me,
because their strength surpasses mine.
8 Out of a dungeon lead me forth,
that I may thank your name.
O how the saints will flock to me,
if you but kindly deal with me!

PSALM 142

Prayers of a Penitent Man Who Is in Dire Straits

I. The psalmist knows that he deserves punishment for his sins,
but he asks God to spare him (1, 2). II. He is depressed, disconsolate. Mindful of God's blessings in other days, he longs again
for God's mercy (3–6). III. He begs for prompt help (7–9). IV. He
asks, moreover, for grace to do God's will (10–12).

1 A psalm of David.

I   Lord, hear my prayer!
You are so faithful — listen to my urgent cry;
you are so just — then answer me!
2 No, do not call your servant to your judgment seat;
no living man is holy in your sight.

141:5. to the right: in a trial, the defender usually stood at the right (cf.
Pss. 15:8; 120:5).
141:8. dungeon: either a cave in which David was confined, as in a dungeon,
or some great affliction, which, metaphorically, might be called a prison.
142:2. The psalmist knows that he is worthy of punishment if God acts
according to strict justice, but he begs for mercy, since all men are sinners
(cf. Pss. 50:6, 7; 129:3).

II **3** A foe is in pursuit of me;
already to the dust he humbled me!
He shut me up in gloom, like one already dead!
4 My spirit in me pines away;
my heart within me has grown numb!
5 But I recall the olden days;
I ponder all your works;
on all your deeds I meditate.
6 My hands — I stretch them out to you;
my soul, like a dried-up land — it thirsts for you.

III **7** Lord, hear me speedily;
my spirit pines away.
O do not hide your face from me;
else I shall be like those descending to the pit.
8 Let me at once receive your grace,
because I trust in you.
Show me the way which I must tread,
because to you I lift my soul.
9 O save me from my foes, O Lord;
in you I put my trust.

IV **10** Teach me to do your will,
because you are my God.
Your Spirit — it is kind!
Let it lead me on even ground.
11 In honor of your name, Lord, keep me safe;
for kind you are; deliver me from my distress.
12 And in your kindness crush my enemies;
and ruin all that vex my soul.
I am your humble worshiper!

142:3c. Deprived of all light and hope, he is like to a man already buried.
142:5. *I recall the olden days:* i.e., the blessings which God conferred upon
the people in past ages. Cf. Ps. 76:4, 6, 12–13.

Psalm 143

Prayers of the King for Victory and Prosperity

I. God, says the king, is the source of all his strength (1, 2). **II.** Conscious of his own unworthiness and weakness, he asks God to stretch forth his hand to help him (3–8). **III.** He promises that, when this danger has been removed, he will gladly sing the praises of God (9–11). **IV.** For the people, the king asks peace, and plenty, in field and flock (12–15).

¹ A psalm of David.

I   Blest be the Lord, my rock,
    who trains my arms for battle, my fingers for the fight,
² my mercy seat, my citadel,
    my garrison, and my deliverer,
    my shield, my safe retreat,
    who subjugates the nations to my sway.

II ³ Lord, what is man, that you should care for him;
    what mortal man, that you should think of him!
⁴ A man is like a breath of air;
    like to a passing shadow are his days!
⁵ Incline your firmament, O Lord; descend;
    touch the mountains and smoke will belch from them;
⁶ flash forth your lightnings: scatter them;
    let fly your shafts: disrupt their ranks.
⁷ Reach out your hand from heaven on high;
    deliver me; and set me free from surging waves, from foreigners'
      hands;
⁸ *their mouth but speaks the lie;*
    and their right hand is raised for perjury.

III ⁹ God, let me sing to you a song not sung before,
    make melody to you upon the ten-stringed harp,
¹⁰ you, who grant to kings the victory —
    you who have helped your servant David to escape.
¹¹ From *deadly sword deliver me,*
    and *set me free from foreigners' hands.*

Their mouth but speaks the lie,
and their right hand is raised for perjury.

IV 12 Our sons — be they like saplings,
    flourishing in their youth;
    our daughters — be they as corner shafts,
    as sculptured columns in a shrine.

 13 Our granaries — be they filled,
    and flowing o'er with every kind of crop;
    our flocks — prodigious be their fruitfulness,
    and multiplied a thousandfold upon our fields;

 14 our burden-beasts — let them be heaped with loads.
    Let there be no breach of wall, no banishment,
    no wailing in our streets.

 15 Well for the race blest in this wise;
    well for the race whose God is the Lord.

PSALM 144

Greatness and Goodness of God

This psalm is alphabetical (cf. Introduction, Ps. 9). The psalmist begins with praise of God (1, 2); he celebrates his majesty and power (3–6), his goodness (7–9), the glory of his kingdom (10–13b), his care and providence over all things (13c–16), his benignity toward good men (17–20). Let all, therefore, bless God's holy name forever (21).

 1 *Praises of David.*

   I will extol you, O my God, my King;
   and bless your name forever and for aye.

 2 Yes, I will bless you every day;
   and praise your name forever and for aye.

 3 Great is the Lord, deserving highest praise;
   his greatness cannot be explored.

 4 Age to age proclaims your works,
   makes known your might.

143:12d. *sculptured columns:* these words seem to describe the beautiful and charming appearance of the daughters. There is no comparison of them with caryatids.

⁵ They tell the mighty splendor of your majesty,
and blaze your wondrous deeds.
⁶ They sing the might of your stupendous works;
they herald your magnificence.

⁷ The praises of your goodness they proclaim,
and in your justice they exult.
⁸ The Lord is kind and merciful,
to anger slow, and full of graciousness.
⁹ The Lord is good to all,
toward all his creatures merciful.

¹⁰ May all your works, Lord, hymn your praise,
and may your holy ones give blessings to you.
¹¹ Let them reveal the glory of your reign,
and praise your might,
¹² to make to mortals known your might
and the transcendent glory of your sway.
¹³ Your reign outlives all time,
and your dominion lasts from age to age.

The Lord is true in all his words,
and holy in all his deeds.
¹⁴ The Lord upholds all those who fall,
and raises up all the depressed.
¹⁵ The eyes of all look hopefully to you,
and in due time you give them food.
¹⁶ You open your hand,
and bountifully sate all living things.

¹⁷ The Lord is just in all his ways,
and holy in all his deeds.
¹⁸ The Lord is near to all who call on him,
to all who call on him sincerely.
¹⁹ And he will grant the wish of those who reverence him,
and hear their cry, and rescue them.
²⁰ The Lord guards all who love him,
but all the godless he destroys.

²¹ O may my mouth proclaim the praises of the Lord,
may all men bless his holy name forever and for aye.

PSALM 145

Praise of God, Eternal King and Helper of All

The psalmist sings God's praise. I. No hope, he says, should be placed in weak men (3, 4). II. Let hope be placed in God (5–10), who created all things (6), who helps the oppressed and the afflicted (7–9), and who will reign eternally (10).

This is the first of five Psalms of Praise, with which the Psalter ends. They are so called because they have as a common theme the praise of God.

1 Alleluia.

O praise, my soul, the Lord!
2 Yes, I will praise the Lord throughout my life;
to my God shall I sing as long as I live.

I   3 No, do not trust in men of rank,
in man, who has no power to save.
4 His spirit passes, and to his dust he must return;
then all his plannings come to nought.

II   5 O well for him whose help is Jacob's God,
whose hope is in the Lord, his God;
6 'tis he made heaven and earth,
the sea and all that is in them.
'Tis he keeps faith eternally;
7 who renders justice to the oppressed,
gives to the hungry bread.
The Lord sets captives free;
8 the Lord opens blind men's eyes;
the Lord lifts up those that are bowed down;
the Lord loves holy men.
9 The Lord shields strangers;
upholds the widow and the fatherless;
but he upsets the sinners' plots.
10 The Lord will reign eternally,
your God, O Sion, from age to age. Alleluia!

PSALMS 146 AND 147
Praise of God, the Mighty and
Wise Restorer of Israel

Psalms 146 and 147 are taken as one psalm; they both have the same theme.

The psalm has three parts. I. Praise of God, the powerful and wise restorer of Israel (1–6). II. Praise of God, who in his providence, governs all things in favor of those who reverence him (7–11). III. Praise of God, who restored the city of Jerusalem, endowed it with peace and prosperity, directs the powers of nature, and gave a law to his people (12–20).

PSALM 146 (1–11)

I   **1** O praise the Lord, for he is good;
     sing to our God, for he is kind.
     Praise is his proper due.

   2 The Lord builds up Jerusalem;
     he gleans the scattered sons of Israel.

   3 He heals the broken hearts;
     he binds their wounds.

   4 'Tis he defines the number of the stars;
     he calls each one by name.

   5 Great is our Lord, and mighty is his strength;
     his wisdom passes measuring.

   6 The Lord upraises humble souls;
     but godless men he humbles to the dust.

II **7** Sing to the Lord and render thanks;
     hymn, to the harp, our God.

   8 With clouds he overspreads the sky,
     prepares the rain for dried-up land.
     He lets the grass grow on the mountainsides,
     and plants, to serve the needs of man.

   9 To cattle he accords their food,
     to the raven's young, that cry to him.

146:9. The parent ravens are said to expel their young from the nest while they are yet very young.

10 He does not take delight in horse's strength,
   nor do man's limbs please him.
11 Those please the Lord that reverence him,
   who in his goodness put their trust.

Psalm 147 (12–20)

III 12 Praise the Lord, Jerusalem;
   Mount Sion, praise your God.
13 He strengthened the bars of your gates,
   and blessed your children in your midst.
14 He settled peace within your borders,
   and filled you with the choicest wheat.
15 He sends his word forth to the earth,
   and swiftly runs his utterance.
16 And snow he gives — like softest wool;
   he scatters ice — like ashes.
17 His hail he flings out — like crumbs of bread;
   the waters freeze beneath his frost.
18 Then he issues his command and thaws them out;
   he bids his wind blow, and the waters flow.
19 To Jacob he declared his word,
   his precepts and decrees to Israel.
20 Not thus did he with any other nation deal;
   nor did he make his precepts known to them.
   Alleluia!

Psalm 148

Let Heaven and Earth Praise the Lord

The psalmist summons all creation to sing, in splendid concert, the praises of the Lord. I. He calls on the heavens, the angels, the stars, the waters (1–6). II. He then turns to the earth (7–12): the sea with its denizens (7), the air (8), the mountains and hills (9a), the trees (9b), the animal kingdom (10), and men of every condition and age (11, 12). God, all-powerful, strengthens his people Israel (13, 14).

146:10, 11. God is pleased, not by mere strength and might, but by faith and trust (cf. Pss. 19:8; 32:16–18).

¹ *Alleluia.*

I   In heaven praise the Lord,
    and praise him in the heights above.
² Praise him, his angels, each and all;
  praise him, his armies, each and all.
³ Praise him, sun and moon,
  praise him, all you shining stars.
⁴ Praise him, heaven of heavens,
  and waters o'er the firmament.
⁵ Let them praise the name of the Lord.
  He issued the command: they came to be.
⁶ He 'stablished them to last for all eternity,
  and gave a law that shall not be annulled.

II ⁷ Praise the Lord upon the earth —
  monsters of the sea and all its deeps;
⁸ fire and hail, and snow and mist,
  and stormy winds, obedient to his word;
⁹ mountains and hillocks, each and all;
  fruit trees and cedars, each and all;
¹⁰ wild beasts and cattle, each and all;
  reptiles, and birds upon the wing;
¹¹ earth's kings and nations, each and all;
  earth's princes and judges, each and all;
¹² young men and maidens too,
  old men, and little boys also.

¹³ Let them praise the name of the Lord:
  transcendent is the name of him alone!
  His majesty transcends both heaven and earth.
¹⁴ Great is the strength which he accords his race.
  O what distinction for his saints,
  the sons of Israel, the people close to him!
  Alleluia!

148:2b. *armies*: the various orders of angels are so designated.
148:4. *heaven of heavens*: highest heavens.

PSALM 149

With Song and Sword Let Israel Praise the Lord

I. The psalmist calls on the Israelites to praise God, who chose them, rules them, loves them, and makes them ever victorious (1–5); II. but he calls on them no less to prepare for battle, prompt to execute the judgment of God on the Gentile kings and nations (6–9).

1   *Alleluia.*

I   Sing to the Lord a song not sung before!
     And let his praise resound wherever saints foregather!
2   Let Israel rejoice in its maker;
     the sons of Sion exult in their king!
3   Let them with dancing praise his name;
     with tambourine and harp make melody to him;
4   because the Lord loves his race,
     and crowns the humble folk with victory.
5   And let the saints be happy in their glory,
     and on their couch be full of joy!

II   6   The eulogies of God be in their mouths;
         and two-edged swords be in their hands:
     7   to wreak revenge upon the Gentiles,
         and punishments upon the tribes;
     8   to bind their kings with shackles,
         their noble men with iron bands;
     9   to execute on them the judgment pre-ordained:
         this is the boast of all his saints. Alleluia.

149:5b. *on their couch:* i.e., enjoying quiet and repose after they have won their victory.

149:7, 8. The reference is to kings and tribes who were enemies of God and the Messias.

Psalm 150

A Solemn Concert of Praise for God

This psalm is the doxology of Book 5 and of the whole Psalter. God is to be praised here on earth in the temple, and in heaven (1), because of his works and majesty (2). In this praise, the whole symphony of the temple's music should join; indeed, everything that breathes should join the chorus of praise (3–5).

1 *Alleluia.*

O praise the Lord within his holy shrine;
praise him in his majestic firmament.
2 Give praise to him for his grand works;
praise him for his transcendent majesty.
3 Give praise to him with blast of horn;
praise him with harp and psaltery.
4 Praise him with tambourine and dance;
praise him with flute and stringed instrument.
5 Praise him with sounding castanets;
with crashing cymbals give him praise.
May every breathing thing give praise to the Lord.
Alleluia!

Father —
Jungalatis
Union 1 - 1500
Epterson 394 Languge Lab
P.C.